MYTHS AND LEGENDS
FROM AROUND THE WORLD

Sowmya Rajendran has written for children of all ages, from picture books to young adult fiction and non-fiction. She, along with her co-author Niveditha Subramaniam, won the Sahitya Akademi's Bal Sahitya Puraskar for her novel *Mayil Will Not Be Quiet!* in 2015. Sowmya grew up in Chennai and lives in Pune. She unfortunately does not have a dog or any exotic pet that she can include in her bio. She enjoys writing with a sense of humour and is interested in looking at stories from underexplored perspectives. Sowmya currently works with The News Minute, writing on gender, culture and cinema.

MYTHS AND LEGENDS
FROM AROUND THE WORLD

SOWMYA RAJENDRAN

RUPA

Published by
Rupa Publications India Pvt. Ltd 2020
7/16, Ansari Road, Daryaganj
New Delhi 110002

Sales centres:
Bengaluru Chennai
Hyderabad Jaipur Kathmandu
Kolkata Mumbai Prayagraj

Copyright © Sowmya Rajendran 2020

All rights reserved.

No part of this publication may be reproduced, transmitted,
or stored in a retrieval system, in any form or by any means,
electronic, mechanical, photocopying, recording or otherwise,
without the prior permission of the publisher.

This is a work of fiction. Names, characters, places and incidents are either the
product of the author's imagination or are used fictitiously and any resemblance
to any actual person, living or dead, events or locales is entirely coincidental.

P-ISBN: 978-93-89967-69-2
E-ISBN: 978-93-89967-71-5

Eighth impression 2024

10 9 8

The moral right of the author has been asserted.

Printed in India

This book is sold subject to the condition that it shall not, by way of
trade or otherwise, be lent, resold, hired out, or otherwise circulated,
without the publisher's prior consent, in any form of binding
or cover other than that in which it is published.

For Adhira

Contents

Creation

1. How Nu Wa Created the World — 3
   A Story from China
2. How the Zebra Got His Stripes — 8
   A Story from the San People of Africa
3. Hermaphroditus — 13
   A Story from Greece
4. How Anansi Brought Stories to the World — 19
   A Story from West Africa
5. How Pangu Created the World — 24
   A Story from China

Conflict

6. Tinirau and Kae — 31
   A Story from the Maori People
7. Perseus and Andromeda — 38
   A Story from Greece
8. Rustom and Sohrab — 43
   A Story from Persia
9. How Lelawala, the Maid of the Mist, Saved Her People — 51
   A Story from the Native Americans
10. Romulus and Remus — 58
    A Story from Rome

11. How Thor Won Back His Hammer — 64
   A Story from the Nordic Countries

12. Amaterasu Hides in the Cave — 71
   A Story from Japan

13. Osiris and Isis — 77
   A Story from Egypt

14. Hippolyta and Theseus — 82
   A Story from Greece

Churning

15. Maveli Goes Home — 93
   A Story from India

16. Renuka, the Warrior Goddess — 99
   A Story from India

17. How Kundalakesa Became a Monk — 105
   A Story from India

18. Andal — 111
   A Story from India

19. Nandanar — 117
   A Story from India

20. Sinhabahu — 122
   A Story from Sri Lanka

21. Cassandra's Prophecy — 128
   A Story from Greece

22. Scheherazade — 135
   A Story from Arabia

Acknowledgements — 143

Creation

ONE

How Nu Wa Created the World

A Story from China

Nu Wa, the goddess, looked around Mount Kunlun. There was beauty wherever her eyes travelled. The snow lay like a blanket upon the earth. The world was quiet, new. Far away, she could see the bears ambling across the hill. The sky was empty of birds. Mount Kunlun was so high that its peak almost touched the sky.

Nu Wa walked down the mountain, through the clouds. As the animals saw her approach, they bent low in respect and made way for her to pass. Nu Wa smiled at them gently; they were her children, each one of them.

When she reached the river, Nu Wa stared at her own reflection. At the majestic face and the dragon-like body. And then she sighed.

The great mother goddess was lonely. She had created the earth, the sky and the four pillars to hold it up. She had created the animals and the birds, but there was something missing. A strange heaviness sat in her chest. Nu Wa couldn't say what exactly was bothering her. Who does a goddess turn to when she is sad?

Her eyes fell upon the yellow clay in the riverbank.

'Could it be?' Nu Wa said to herself. She sat down and began kneading the clay. She made little forms that looked just like her but with a different body. No dragon tail for these babies, she told herself. Just her face would do, and the body would be inspired by the big monkeys.

When the goddess's breath fell upon the forms, they took life and rose. They danced away into the distance as Nu Wa watched, faintly amused.

She made many more little figures. She gave some long hair, some short hair and some no hair at all. One got eyes that crinkled when she smiled, another a frown so deep it turned his forehead into a valley. Nu Wa had not enjoyed herself like this in a while.

But then, she lost her patience. This was taking too long! There was so much clay, after all. Nu Wa knew just what to do. She grabbed a branch from a tree and dipped it into the river. Then, she shook the droplets off the branch and they fell on the earth, far and near.

Each little droplet turned into a person. And that's how people were born all over the world.

Now there was song, now there was dance, and now, Nu Wa no longer felt lonely. From her home in the mountain, she watched over her latest creations, the human beings who never failed to entertain her with their antics.

Years passed. The people lived in harmony with each other. But the earth took on a life of its own.

Sometimes, fires broke out that charred whole forests to a silken black. Nu Wa watched sadly as the animals ran to escape the hungry flames.

'Should I stop the fire?' Nu Wa wondered. But if she did, should she step in whenever any of her children were in distress?

What if a fawn called out to her when the tiger was about to pounce on it?

What if the bees buzzed their unhappiness when humans tore down their hives for honey?

What if the trees found the birds too heavy to bear?

And what if the tiger complained that the fawn had escaped and his stomach rumbled?

After creating them all, Nu Wa had allowed them to work out their own balance. She gave the lion its mane and sharp claws, but she also gave the rabbit fast legs. Who won and who lost everyday battles, she did not keep count.

But it was not easy.

Once, when a flood rose, carrying away a village, Nu Wa observed a mother and a baby struggling in the water. She helped them then, sending a log of wood their way. But she didn't want to do it always.

Now, as she looked up at the sky, a shiver went down

her spine. It was dark as night, though it was only noon. Thunder sounded deep in the woods. The wind blew so hard that Nu Wa could feel her hair flying.

And then, as she watched in horror, it seemed as if the sky would be ripped into two. Such was the ferocity of the storm. The rain fell in sheets and Nu Wa knew the river would rise to gobble up everything in its path.

But that was the least of her worries. The four pillars that held up the sky were shaking!

'No!' shouted Nu Wa. She would not allow the earth to be destroyed.

But before the mother goddess could do anything, the pillars crashed to the earth—one after the other. The sky split into two and broke the earth.

Screams. Screams everywhere. Nu Wa was blinded by tears. How could she allow this to happen? She saw that the earth was slipping, about to fall into an abyss.

For a moment, Nu Wa thought it was all over. Then, she shut her eyes and willed herself to stay calm. She could fix this. She had to.

Nu Wa conjured up a fire and melted together the five coloured stones. Blue, red, yellow, white and black. Each of them stood for the five elements—wood, fire, earth, metal and water. The stones bubbled in the fire, the liquids running into each other and forming again.

Nu Wa lifted up the broken sky and patched it together with the material made of the five stones. It took her nine days, but in the end, the sky was back in place, strong and unshakable.

Then, Nu Wa asked the giant tortoise for help. She needed him to save the earth. The tortoise was only too happy to help his mother. Nu Wa chopped off his legs and used them as the four pillars.

She went around the earth putting out fires and healing her beloved creations. For when the children call out in pain, can the mother turn her face away?

In Chinese mythology, Nu Wa is the mother goddess who created the earth and all life forms. She is described as having a human face with the body of the dragon. Most cultures around the world have an origin story to explain how the earth was created. Many have similar elements—the Creator making humans in his/her own image, the arrival of a flood, and how the Supreme One took the help of animals to save the earth. The five elements, according to Chinese mythology, are wood, fire, earth, metal and water.

TWO

How the Zebra Got His Stripes

A Story from the San People of Africa

The land was dry as a bone. The cracks looked like sharp shadows of great trees falling upon the ground. Zebra was worried. His little son was prancing about without a care in the world, but Zebra knew that tough times lay ahead.

The last time the drought had been upon them, Zebra had been quite young. But he could still remember how much the herd had suffered. His father, grown weak and tired, had told him to keep going till he found another river. He was going to rest for a while and join his son. But Zebra never saw him after that. Did a lion catch him? Or did he just die of thirst? He did not want to find out.

'Dad! Come and look at this!' his son called out.

Zebra smiled in spite of himself. The little one was always showing him his 'discoveries'. A light-coloured rock, an orange butterfly, the way the grass danced...

Zebra's eyes fell on the grass. It was withered brown. A fire could start so easily…

'DAD!' his son's impatient voice made him look up. 'Look what I found!' he said.

Zebra stared. It was a beautiful green beetle. It was dead, but he didn't want to tell his son that. 'Come on, we must go on a trip,' he said instead.

'Where?' asked his son, his eyes growing round with excitement.

Zebra didn't quite know the answer yet, so he said, 'It's a surprise!'

'Are we going to see Mama?' asked the little one.

His father looked at him sadly. The little one's mother had been hunted down by Man, but Zebra had not told him the truth yet.

'Just some place. You'll know when you see it,' Zebra said.

Many from the herd had already left. Zebra had waited for so long because he was not sure if his son could make the journey. Or if, at the end of it, they would find the river. His uncle had told him that it was around the big mountain, but nobody knew for sure. No one had travelled that far until now.

Zebra and the little one kept walking. His son chattered on. Did Papa know that at night, when there was no light at all, not even the moonlight, there were tiny insects that came out glowing like fire? His friend had told him that these were fireflies. But it didn't hurt to touch them. And did Papa know that in the river, the one that was now almost dry, there was a giant fish that was bigger than his snout? Did Papa know that an ostrich couldn't fly though it was a bird? Silly Papa did not know anything!

Zebra grinned with affection. Oh, what wouldn't he give to see his son grow tall and strong!

Suddenly, the little one paused. 'Look! Look at that yellow bird!' he said and dashed away from his father, into the bush.

'Wait!' Zebra called out in panic.

But the little one was gone. Zebra ran after him.

What was this? Ahead of him lay a glittering pool. Quiet and green, from the reflection of the trees that shielded it.

'Look, Papa, it's a pool!' said his son happily.

But just as Zebra was about to take a step towards the water, to drink to his heart's content, he heard a deep voice.

'Go away! I'm the Lord of the Water and this is my kingdom!'

It was a giant Baboon who was sitting by a fire. His hairy face was fierce as a lion's.

The little one giggled when he heard this, but Zebra was not amused.

'The water belongs to all. Nobody can say it's theirs alone,' Zebra shot back.

'I can!' said Baboon, getting up from the fire. He was even bigger than Zebra had thought. He caught the sudden fear on his son's face.

'We're in the middle of a drought. It's not fair that you don't share the water,' Zebra said calmly. 'Don't you care about the animals who are dying?'

Baboon shrugged. 'This water is mine,' he repeated, slowly moving towards Zebra.

Zebra stood firm. He was not going to let Baboon bully him. 'Be reasonable,' Zebra said. 'Let's not make this ugly.'

But Baboon was in no mood to listen to reason. With a swing, he landed on Zebra's back and began pummelling him.

'STOP! STOP!' shouted the little one. But Baboon barely heard him.

Zebra wasn't going to give up so easily though. He heaved himself and shook until Baboon landed with a crash on the ground. But the fight was far from over. Even as the little one screamed in terror, Zebra and Baboon kicked and scratched, dodged and punched. The birds in the trees flew away in fright.

At last, Zebra kicked Baboon so hard that the giant monkey flew high into the sky and landed amongst the rocks. So much so that his bottom turned red.

Zebra was very tired, but he was happy he had won. He'd found water! He could tell his herd, he could save everyone!

In his joy, Zebra did not notice where he was going. He fell on Baboon's fire, scorching his beautiful white coat. His panicked son gathered water in his mouth and threw it into the fire to quench it. But it was too late—Zebra's coat had black stripes all over it.

'Let's go back!' said the little one. 'Look, it's starting to rain!'

And indeed, it was. Zebra looked up at the darkening sky, the grey clouds racing across the blue expanse. Rain was here.

Zebra and son went back to their home in the plains. For now, the battle was over. But Zebra knew that Baboon would never forget him. That's why even today, zebras have black stripes. As for the baboons, they still have red bottoms and walk with their tails up to ease the pain!

This story comes from the San people of Africa, who are made up of various hunter-gatherer groups. The San people are also called Bushmen and are from Southern Africa. There are many such stories about animals and why they are the way they are. You will find that people all over the world have come up with such explanations for the animals and birds that they see around them.

THREE

Hermaphroditus

A Story from Greece

Hermaphroditus was a beautiful young man, born to Hermes, the messenger of the gods, and Aphrodite, the goddess of love and beauty. But not long after he was born, he was given away to the nymphs who lived in Mount Ida. It was just as well, for his parents were busy gods who had little time to indulge his many questions. The nymphs, on the other hand, doted on him.

As a boy, Hermaphroditus loved climbing up and down the formidable mountain where Zeus had been hidden away as a baby to stop his father, Cronus, from killing him. Hermaphroditus knew every crevice, every stone, every twig that grew on the rocky surface. But as he grew older, Hermaphroditus wished to leave the sacred mountain and explore the world.

'I want to go where the eagles fly,' he told the nymphs.

'I want to dive into the ocean, see the stars shining in rivers that I have only dreamt of, visit strange islands with mythical beasts.'

The nymphs tried to stop him from leaving, but he wouldn't listen to their pleas. At last, they kissed his forehead and wished him well.

'Will he be safe?' asked one nymph to the other.

'With his beauty, he can conquer the world,' the companion replied, her heart filled with pride as she watched the strapping young man climb down the mountain briskly.

And indeed, Hermaphroditus found that his striking good looks made people trust him easily. He had no trouble at all getting food or accommodation wherever he went.

'He looks like a god!' the people whispered to each other, eager to please him just so he would flash his charming smile at them.

Hermaphroditus was flattered and amused by all the attention. He wandered around Lycia, where he'd reached after several days of travel, enjoying being the mysterious stranger who aroused everyone's curiosity.

That night, Hermaphroditus sat by a lake, watching the moon float in the water. He missed home, but not for a moment did he regret his decision to leave. How much had he seen in these past few days! And how much had he feasted and made merry!

Just then, he noticed an old man hobbling towards him.

'Stranger, what brings you to Lycia?' asked the old man,

when his eyes fell upon Hermaphroditus.

'Wanderlust,' said the young man, shrugging.

The old man smiled, settling down next to Hermaphroditus. 'I set out in my youth like you once. A journey of 101 days. Ah, the places I saw!' he said, with a sigh.

The wrinkles on his face looked like delicate cobwebs, but his eyes were still full of light.

'Tell me about them,' said Hermaphroditus, hugging his knees. He looked forward to charting his course on the map that he had in his satchel.

'If I tell you about them, it will be several nights before we rise,' the old man laughed. 'But have you been to the woods near Halicarnassus yet?'

Hermaphroditus shook his head. 'No, where is that?' he asked, curious.

'In Caria,' replied the old man. 'There is a pool there that is the most beautiful place I have seen.'

'Really?' said Hermaphroditus. Caria was not far from Lycia and already, he was planning on how to get there.

The old man got up and bade goodbye to Hermaphroditus. He was humming a song in a language that the young man did not understand.

The next day, Hermaphroditus left for Caria. He walked half the way and then managed to get into a horse cart travelling along the same route.

When he reached the woods, he was a little disappointed. It didn't seem all that special. It wasn't even as big as some of the woods he'd seen in the past few days. Nevertheless, he made his way inside, hoping that the old man was right.

The trees became taller and broader as he went in deeper. And at last, he saw it. At the heart of the woods, there was a small, glittering pool, lit up by the feeble rays of the sun that had managed to pierce through the trees.

The water was a shade of blue-green that he had never seen before. It reminded him of his mother Aphrodite's eyes. Mesmerized, Hermaphroditus was about to step into the water when a sharp voice rang out, 'Who are you, stranger? And what is your business here?'

It was Salmacis, a nymph who lived by the pool. But even as Hermaphroditus was about to answer, he noticed that the nymph no longer appeared angry. Instead, she was staring at him open-mouthed.

'I'm Hermaphroditus,' he said hesitantly. He did not understand why Salmacis was looking at him like that.

'You're the most beautiful young man I've ever seen!' Salmacis exclaimed.

Hermaphroditus blushed furiously, but he was pleased. 'And you are?' he asked.

'Salmacis,' she replied, moving towards him.

But as she came closer, Hermaphroditus felt uncomfortable. He sensed danger from this strange woman, beautiful as she was.

'I'm leaving,' he said, hastily putting on his clothes.

Salmacis didn't listen. She was so struck by Hermaphroditus

that no other thought entered her mind. When the young man tried to move away, Salmacis was so desperate to make him stay that she climbed on his back and clung to him!

'Let me go!' shouted Hermaphroditus, but Salmacis wouldn't listen.

'Say you will stay with me!' Salmacis shouted back.

Hermaphroditus shook this way and that, trying to get Salmacis off his back, but the nymph held on tightly, as if she were a crab and her hands were pincers.

'Do you plan to stay on my back forever?' called out Hermaphroditus. 'Because the second you get down, I will leave. This isn't my home.'

When Salmacis heard this, she called out to the gods. 'By the powers that be, let Hermaphroditus and me forever be one!' she said.

The trees shook and the pool rippled. The birds on the trees fell quiet. And wonders of wonders, Salmacis merged into Hermaphroditus's body.

'That is not what I meant!' shrieked the nymph. 'I wanted to stay...'

But before she could complete her sentence, she had dissolved into Hermaphroditus.

The young man glanced at his body in amazement. He was now both man and woman. He ran to the pool and looked at his reflection. His face, too, was changed.

Hermaphroditus wept. He no longer recognized himself. His salty tears mixed with the clear water of the pool, making the fish swim around his legs in circles.

But as the hours passed, Hermaphroditus felt a quiet strength within him. There was nobody else in the world who was like him—to have this form, to know what it meant to be part man, part woman. He got up, wiping his tears away.

'From now on, whoever enters this pool shall become like me, and I will be their leader. May the gods make my words come true,' he said.

And they did.

While the world we live in today sees sex as male or female, nature offers a lot more diversity. Hermaphroditus, who came to have the physical features of a man and a woman, has been celebrated as the symbol of androgyny for centuries. Androgyny is a combination of characteristics that are associated with the masculine and the feminine, thereby not falling into the neat boxes that society has drawn for us. Hindu mythology speaks of the Ardhanareeshwara form, a combination of Shiva and Parvathy, which is also meant to symbolize the union of masculine and feminine energies.

FOUR

How Anansi Brought Stories to the World

A Story from West Africa

A long time ago, there were no stories in the world. Nobody made up tales about fantastic beasts or magical beings who roamed the skies. No stories to make the children laugh when they were sad, no stories to scare the grown-ups as they sat around the fire at night, eating their food.

As there were no stories to hold them together, people forgot where they came from and who they were. Who was Grandpa? How did Grandma smile? What did the river where Papa used to swim look like? Was Mama's hair always so long? The time when the lion came to the village, how did the elders drive him away?

Nobody knew because people had no stories to tell.

It was Nyan-Konpon, the sky god, who had all the stories in the world. But he was selfish and did not want to share them.

One day, Kwaku Anansi, the spider, went to the sky god to buy his stories. Anansi was known as a troublemaker, but he also helped people once in a while, when he was in the mood for it.

When he went to Nyan-Konpon, he bent low and greeted him. 'I've come from far to see you. I want to buy your stories,' he said.

'What makes you think I'm going to sell the stories to you?' Nyan-Konpon said, bursting into laughter.

Nyan-Konpon told him that many people had come from great towns to buy his stories, but that he'd never budged.

Anansi, however, was confident about his ability to persuade Nyan-Konpon. 'Everything has a price. Tell me how much your stories cost,' he said.

Nyan-Konpon was amused by the audacity of the spider. He thought for a while and said, 'My stories can be bought if you bring me Onini the python, Osebo the leopard, Mmoboro the hornet and Mmoatia the fairy.'

Nyan-Konpon was sure that Anansi would throw his legs up in the air and say that this was not possible, but the spider merely smiled. 'I will do as you say and bring them all,' he said.

The sky god simply pretended to yawn and nodded his head.

Now, Anansi had to come up with tricks to get all those the sky god wanted in exchange for the stories.

First, he went to where Onini, the giant python, lived.

He was long and thick, with glittering black diamonds on his back. Anansi knew that the python was very proud of his size.

And so, the clever spider said loudly, 'I know Onini is long and there's nobody longer than him. But my wife Aso says that he's not even as long as the branch of a palm tree!'

Hearing this, Onini rose from the branch of the tree where he was resting and hissed. 'I'm indeed longer than the branch of a palm tree!' he said in anger.

Anansi shrugged and said, 'Let's test that out then.'

He told the python that he must stretch himself out against the branch to prove his claim. When Onini did so, Anansi said, 'But you must be absolutely straight! Here, let me tie you up with this rope so you don't curl up and we can really see your size.'

Foolish Onini agreed and in no time, Anansi captured him. He took the python to the sky god. Nyan-Konpon was surprised, but he was sure that Anansi would fail with the others.

'The leopard! Ha, you'll never catch the leopard!' declared Nyan-Konpon.

But, Anansi had a plan for Osebo too. When the leopard was out hunting, Anansi dug a deep hole in the ground. Osebo fell inside and growled in rage.

Anansi went close to the hole and said, 'Oh no! Osebo, I must get you out. Here, let me spin a web for you. You hold onto it and come out.'

Poor Osebo did not see through Anansi's cunning and

allowed himself to be trapped in the web. Once Anansi lifted him out of the hole, off he took him to Nyan-Konpon.

This time, the sky god was a bit nervous, but he still did not lose hope that Anansi would fail in the next two tasks. 'You have to get me Mmoboro the hornet. He's no simpleton to fall for your tricks!' said the sky god.

Anansi knew just what to do. He went near the hornet's nest with a calabash filled with water. He poured some of it over a banana leaf that he held over his head and the hornet's nest.

'It's raining, it's raining!' Anansi shouted.

When the hornet came out of his nest, he saw the water droplets falling out of the banana leaf and believed Anansi.

'Get into this calabash and you will be safe,' said the spider.

When the hornet got inside, Anansi quickly closed the calabash and took it to the sky god.

Nyon-Konpon was shocked to see the hornet. But, he still wouldn't give up. 'Mmoatia the fairy is clever. She will never believe your lies!' said the sky god.

Anansi knew that what Nyon-Konpon said was true. Mmoatia was indeed a clever fairy. And so, to catch her, he made a doll and covered it with gum. He knew that Mmoatia had a temper and this was his best shot. He put the doll under a tree where the fairies played and also put some yam in a bowl in front of it.

When Mmoatia came to play, she saw the bowl and was

immediately tempted. She ate up the yam and thanked the doll, thinking it was another fairy. When the doll did not respond, Mmoatia thought her to be rude.

'Can't you answer when someone thanks you?' asked the angry fairy.

When the doll still said nothing, Mmoatia hit her. But oh no, her hands were now stuck to the doll!

Anansi quickly grabbed the doll and Mmoatia and took them to the sky god.

When Nyon-Konpon saw Anansi, his shoulders slumped. The trickster spider had indeed won the challenge fair and square.

'Well done, Anansi!' said the sky god. 'I present to you all my stories. From now on, they will be known as yours and not the sky god's stories!'

The delighted Anansi ran back to earth with the stories and since then, the people have always had a tale to tell when they met each other.

Anansi is a recurring character in several West African and Caribbean stories. He is considered to be the spirit of all knowledge of stories. The name 'Anansi' means 'spider' in Akan, the language spoken by the Ashanti people of Ghana who are credited with creating the character. Anansi often takes the form of a 'trickster', a character in folktales who is clever and amoral, and uses his wits to get what he wants. Anansi became a symbol of resistance and inspiration for the African people who were taken as slaves in real life, because of his ability to get the better of those more powerful than him.

FIVE

How Pangu Created the World

A Story from China

*I*n the beginning, there was nothing. There was no sun, there was no moon. There were no stars shining in the sky.

There was no sky.

There was nobody on earth to look up at the sky in wonder.

There was no earth.

The universe was full of chaos. It had not yet understood how to put things in order.

For thousands of years, the universe was churning. And at last, in the end, the chaos—which had no form until then—shaped itself into a giant egg. This is the giant egg from where you came. From where I came. From where all of us came.

Thus 18,000 years passed. It was a long time for an egg

to hatch. A hen's egg hatches in twenty-one days. An emu's takes about fifty days. A crocodile's takes about eighty days. But if it took 18,000 years for *this* egg to hatch, it was because it was so huge and had within it someone very special.

Now in these 18,000 years, the universe had done a lot of thinking. And the end result of this thinking was Pangu.

Pangu was the large giant who'd been asleep all these years in the egg. It was now time for him to wake up. He stirred inside the egg and broke open the shell. Not little by little like a baby bird, but all at once. CRACK! He squeezed himself out to take a good look at the universe.

'Hmm!' said Pangu, rubbing his eyes open. Outside the egg, it was not so warm and cozy, so the hair on Pangu's body grew to make him feel comfortable. He also wore a coat of fur.

He touched his head, feeling the horns on them. They were curved and sharp.

'Hmm!' said Pangu again. In his hand was an axe. Pangu swung it with full force. A loud noise echoed across the universe. Suddenly, Pangu could see the blue sky over him and the brown earth below him.

Excited, Pangu ran over the earth in joy. But what was this? The sky was falling! If Pangu allowed it to crash on the earth, then both would vanish once again.

With all his strength, the giant pushed the sky up again. 'HEAVVVVEEE HOOO!' he shouted, holding the sky up. He stretched his arms as wide as he could to hold up the two ends of the sky. He held it all day, from the time when the sky was a bright blue to the time it turned into an inky black. Each time the sky threatened to come crashing down, Pangu held it up higher and higher.

'Let me come down!' the sky pleaded.

But Pangu shook his head. 'Your place is up there,' he said firmly.

Each day, the sky moved ten feet away from the earth and the earth grew ten feet thicker. Pangu too grew ten feet taller, to hold the sky up.

'HEAAAVVVEEEE HOOO!' he would shout, every single day.

Pangu did this for another 18,000 years. 18,000 years of watching the sun turn blue-orange-black-orange-and-blue again. Along the way, four beasts helped him in his task: Turtle, Qilin, Phoenix and Dragon.

When Pangu had a cold, they held up the sky so he could blow his nose. When the sky grew restless and shifted this way and that, making it impossible for Pangu to hold it up by himself, all of them did it together.

Turtle had a hard shell, Qilin had a single horn, Phoenix had the power to rise again when it grew weak and Dragon could breathe fire to keep them all warm.

Pangu's friends cheered him when he was down. 'You can do it, Pangu!' they would say, whenever his shoulders sagged.

You can imagine how sore Pangu's arms were! At the

end of 18,000 years, the sky stopped trying to tumble down to the earth.

'I will stay where I am,' the sky promised Pangu.

With a groan, Pangu dropped his arms. Ah! It felt good to be free of the burden at last!

But by now, Pangu was very old. His beautiful black hair had turned white. His right eye had grown cloudy. His bones creaked as he took a step, and then another. 'I am finished,' he told Turtle, Qilin, Phoenix and Dragon.

His friends were sad, but they knew they had to let Pangu go. Pangu lay down and shut his eyes. For 18,000 years, he'd been here, in this place. He hated to go just when the sky had at last learnt to behave itself. But Pangu also knew that this was not the end. It was only another beginning.

The breath went out of Pangu's great body. WHOOOSH! His breath became the wind that blew across the world, for the first time ever. It rose up and formed the mist and the clouds.

As he died, Pangu groaned for one last time. The sound reverberated in the sky. We know it today as thunder.

Pangu's left eye, the one which was still bright, became the sun. The cloudy right eye became the moon.

His head, his beautiful giant head, became the mountains. His blood became the rivers; the muscles turned into land where trees would grow.

Remember, Pangu was a very hairy giant? All the body hair turned into the stars. His fur became the forests. His bones became the earth's minerals. The marrow inside the bones turned into precious, beautiful diamonds.

The sweat on his body became the rain that poured on the earth and gave way to life. The fleas in his fur coat became the animals that scurried away to explore the earth.

Pangu's work was done.

Pangu is a creation myth from China. Have you seen the Yin and Yang symbol, which is half black and half white? In Chinese philosophy, it symbolizes that opposite forces are actually part of each other and one cannot exist without the other. Can light exist if we didn't know the dark? Could courage exist if there was no fear? Pangu had Yin and Yang in perfect balance within him and he split the two forces by swinging his axe—creating the gritty earth and the clear sky. Science, of course, has very different explanations for the origin of the earth and other bodies, but it's interesting to see the similarities between the Pangu story and the Big Bang Theory (the explanation that the universe began with a huge mass concentrated at one point that exploded and expanded over the years).

Conflict

SIX

Tinirau and Kae

A Story from the Maori People

Chief Tinirau's home in the sacred island of Motutapu had a guest—Kae, the priest, who had travelled from far away for the birth ceremony of Tuhuruhuru, the chief's son. Tinirau had gone all the way to Kae's home in another island to fetch him for the ceremony.

Hinauri, the chief's wife, was exhausted after the long night of labour, but the couple was greatly pleased with their little son, who smiled a lot and tugged at Hinauri's hair whenever she bent down to kiss him.

Happy too were Tinirau's pets, the whales. Especially Tutunui, his favourite. He leapt in the sea to make the new baby laugh, as Hinauri sat in the yard, nursing him.

'Thank you for your services, Kae,' Tinirau said, and he meant it.

Hinauri nodded. The ceremony had been flawless and she was pleased that Tuhuruhuru had not cried at all. He'd sat with a solemn expression on his face, as if he knew exactly what was going on.

'I will take your leave if you will pay me my fee. My home is a long way off,' Kae replied.

'Of course,' said Tinirau. He went to Tutunui and cut off a piece from the whale's back. Hinauri rushed to apply some herbs on the wound though she knew Tutunui didn't mind the pain.

Whale meat was a popular delicacy among the people and Tinirau thought Kae would be happy with the gift.

'Thank you,' said Kae, but he did not turn back.

'Would you also like a canoe to go back home?' asked Hinauri when she saw Kae hesitating. She didn't want the priest to be upset about anything. Not in her home.

'Actually, I was wondering if I could ride the whale back home? It's very far and it will be tiring to row the canoe by myself,' said Kae.

Tinirau was taken aback when he heard the request. But Kae stared back at him with innocent, wide eyes and he didn't know what else to do than agree.

'All right,' said Tinirau. 'But when you near the shore, get off him and let him swim away. Otherwise, he will be beached.'

Kae put his hands up in the air, as if to say he understood Tinirau's concerns entirely.

'Of course, of course,' he said. 'I will make sure that no harm comes to him.'

Hinauri was uneasy about the exchange. Kae, who had looked respectable and harmless thus far, suddenly appeared cunning to her eyes. When he grinned at her, she noticed that he had crooked teeth. It only made her feel worse. But the promise had been made and she didn't want to say anything more.

And so, Kae sat astride Tutunui and off they went. The whale swam through the water, more graceful than any canoe. As the breeze caressed Kae's sunburnt cheeks, for a moment he felt sorry for the beast. For, Kae had no intention of letting Tutunui return.

As the shore approached, Tutunui slowed down. But Kae held on to the whale, forcing him to swim closer and closer to the land. Soon, it was too late for Tutunui to turn back. His great body hit the shore with the waves and when the water receded, the beast was left gasping on the land.

'You have served me well in your life and you will serve my people well in your death,' said Kae.

The village rejoiced to see the whale lying on the beach. His meat would feed them for weeks!

The poor animal was cut up and cooked in fires that the villagers stoked on the beach.

In his island, Tinirau waited anxiously for Tutunui to return. 'He should have been here by now,' he said to his wife.

Hinauri said nothing, but she knew that Tutunui wasn't coming back.

When twilight fell, Tinirau was furious. 'He has cheated us!' he bellowed. 'Kae has broken his promise!'

'Hush,' said Hinauri. 'You will wake the baby up.'

But she too was angry. Tutunui was beloved to all of them and she missed the dear whale deeply.

'I know what to do,' she told her husband, who was pacing up and down the yard.

He looked up at her questioningly. It was a dark night and the beads around Hinauri's neck gleamed under the moon, which peeked at them from behind the clouds.

'If you go, you will start a war. Innocent people will die,' said Hinauri.

Tinirau knew this was true.

'I will go. With my women,' said Hinauri. 'We will bring him to you. Here.'

Tinirau nodded. Kae would not suspect anything if a group of women arrived at his village.

And so, in the morning, Hinauri and the other women of the tribe dressed up as dancers and got ready to leave.

'Look after him well,' she said, handing over Tuhuruhuru to Tinirau.

The little baby gurgled as Hinauri got into her canoe and began rowing towards Kae's village.

After several hours, the women reached the island and jumped off their canoes. Tutunui's skeleton lay on the sand, with children running in between the bones and playing catch.

A lump rose in Hinauri's throat when she saw the bones, but she pretended that the sand had gotten into her eye and looked away.

The people of the village were delighted to know that the dancers had come to entertain them.

'Where is Kae? How will we ever find him in this crowd?' one of the women whispered to Hinauri.

'He's the one with the crooked teeth. Keep an eye out,' she hissed back.

When everyone had gathered on the beach, the women began to dance. The people clapped along as they sang, shaking their hips and flinging their arms with gay abandon.

Hinauri danced too, but she was watching the crowd with keen eyes.

Was that Kae, sitting next to the woman with yellow beads? Or was it him there, letting his hands run through the sand?

As she twisted and turned, Hinauri thought she saw a familiar face. There! Behind the man in red—was that not Kae?

Hinauri made her way through the crowd, dancing faster and faster. The people parted and let her pass, appreciating her moves.

When she came close to the man, Hinauri sang loudly and pranced around him to make him smile. But the man sat stone-faced.

Was it really Kae? Hinauri wanted to be absolutely sure. The other dancers sensed what she was doing and they too surrounded the man and began dancing.

Louder and louder their voices grew, and faster and faster they moved. At last, when Hinauri bent backwards and her head touched the ground, the man broke into a smile. He had crooked teeth. It was Kae! Luckily, he did not recognize Hinauri in her costume.

After the dance, Hinauri took note of where Kae went. When the village fell silent, she and the other women carried a sleeping Kae into Hinauri's canoe.

'Well done, all of you,' said Hinauri.

The women smiled back at her, proud at what they had accomplished together.

When they reached Motutapu, they carried Kae to a home that looked just like his own in the village.

At dawn, when Kae awoke, he saw Tinirau sitting before him.

'What are you doing here?' he asked, confused. Kae did not realize that he'd been brought to Tinirau's island overnight. He called out for help but to no avail.

'Nobody will come to help you,' said Tinirau. 'Just as nobody helped my beloved Tutunui.'

And with that, Tinirau sank his knife into Kae's heart, avenging the death of the innocent whale.

There are different versions to the story of Finirau and Kae. In some, Kae is a magician while in others, he arrives in Finirau's island by accident. The Maori people are an indigenous tribe in New Zealand. In Patea, a town in New Zealand, you will find the large sculpture of a whale skeleton that was created by artist Kim Jarrett in 2006. It's known as 'The Garden of Tutunui', after the whale who features in this story. The myth doesn't end with Kae's death. His people kill Tuhuruhuru and Finirau unleashes a war upon them to seek revenge.

SEVEN

Perseus and Andromeda

A Story from Greece

Perseus was returning home after his great battle against Medusa in the island of Sarpedon. The Gorgon's head lay in his hands as he flew over the seas on his winged horse. Though dead, Medusa was still dangerous. Anyone staring at her face would instantly turn to stone.

Far below, on the earth, a young woman was tied to the rocks on the shore. She screamed in rage, trying to free herself. But the knots were tight and her hands bled as the ropes rubbed against her skin.

Andromeda, the princess of Ethiopia, was furious but helpless as she awaited her fate.

Her parents, King Cepheus and Queen Cassiopeia, watched the scene from a tower, swallowed by grief. They waited with dread for the moment when the terrible beast would appear on the horizon and drag their daughter into the sea.

'It's my fault,' Cassiopeia wept as Cepheus tried to console her. 'I shouldn't have said something so silly!'

Cepheus let her cry as he held her close to his chest.

Andromeda was dear to both of them but Cassiopeia, especially, adored their daughter. She'd fallen in love with Andromeda even before she had seen her face, tracing the baby's movements in her pregnant belly and singing her lullabies under the moonlight.

One day, when Cassiopeia saw Andromeda in the palace gardens, her long, dark hair streaming down her shoulders and her face lit up by the mellow evening sun, she had declared that Andromeda was the most beautiful woman ever.

'Even more beautiful than the sea nymphs?' her smiling hairdresser had asked her as she braided Cassiopeia's hair by the window.

'Even more beautiful than all of them put together!' Cassiopeia had said, laughing.

Cassiopeia had not imagined then what their banter would bring. The skies immediately darkened as the offended nereids, the sea nymphs, swam to Poseidon, God of the Sea.

'Cassiopeia must suffer!' the sea nymphs had screeched to Poseidon. 'She has insulted us gravely!'

Poseidon did not need any encouragement to rise from his seat and start a storm. He'd been itching to do so for a while anyway. He made the waters rise. The waves grew larger and larger, crashing upon the shore in fury. Thunder rolled in the skies and lighting struck down ancient trees, starting fires all over the country. The people were terrified. What was happening?

The worried Cepheus prayed to Zeus, the all-powerful, to help his people.

'You will have to perform a sacrifice,' Zeus said, 'Only that will appease Poseidon.'

'What must I do?' asked Cepheus, his voice trembling.

Zeus shrugged. Cepheus knew the answer already.

When Cassiopeia heard what Zeus had told Cepheus, she beat her breast and sobbed.

'Let them take me. Not Andromeda! She has done no wrong!' she pleaded.

But Cepheus shook his head. 'They want Andromeda. Nobody else will do.'

When Andromeda heard the news, she tossed her head in anger. 'I must die for so ridiculous a reason? Because I'm beautiful?' she asked. 'Can a mother not admire her daughter? Are the nereids so insecure?'

But as she paced in her room, she could see the devastation below. The light had gone out in the sky and the entire kingdom looked grey—as if it belonged to the dead.

She allowed herself to be tied to the rocks for the sake of her people. But as she waited for Cetus, the sea monster who was swimming towards her, to end her life once and for all, Andromeda pulled against the ropes in a bid to free herself and fight to her last breath. She knew she was going to die, but she would not go down quietly.

Meanwhile, Perseus, who was flying over Andromeda's land, suddenly found himself in the middle of the storm. As the wind tore around him and the spray from the sea hit his heels, Perseus looked down, puzzled. He tried to calm his horse, and it was then that he saw Andromeda, who was writhing against the rocks. Perseus immediately descended.

'Who are you and why are you here?' he asked the princess.

'I could ask you the same question!' replied Andromeda, looking at the winged horse in wonder.

Perseus was amused in spite of himself. He told her who he was—the son of Zeus and Danae, who had built the kingdom of Mycenae.

'And what is it that you are holding behind your back?' asked Andromeda.

'A Gorgon's head,' said Perseus. 'I'm sure it would be wonderful to have a chat but right now, you seem to be in a spot of trouble. Why don't you tell me about that?'

Andromeda smiled. She told him all that had happened. Suddenly, both of them saw the sea parting into two. Cetus was almost there.

With a slash of his sword, Perseus freed Andromeda. And then, as Cetus drew to the shore, the thorny spikes on his back high as a mountain range, Perseus told Andromeda to close her eyes. 'Trust me,' he whispered.

Andromeda did as she was told.

Careful not to look at the head in his hand, Perseus held

it aloft. Greedy Cetus crashed into the shore, eager to eat Andromeda. But the giant beast was turned to stone as its eyes fell upon Medusa's head.

Suddenly, the sea fell quiet. The sky brightened again and the rain that had been beating mercilessly against the earth, stopped.

King Cepheus and Queen Cassiopeia, who had seen it all from the tower, ran to the shore. Cassiopeia pulled Andromeda into her arms, kissing her daughter and mumbling her thanks to Perseus.

'The next time you want to express your love for me, Mother, just buy me a pony or a diamond,' said Andromeda as the relieved Cassiopeia laughed along.

Perseus is said to have killed Medusa on the order of King Polydectes, who wished to marry Perseus's mother. Medusa was one of the three Gorgon sisters who are sometimes described as beautiful and sometimes as monstrous. Medusa had the ability to turn whoever looked at her into stone, but Perseus finally managed to defeat her by looking at her reflection on his shield and fighting her. In some versions of the Andromeda story, Perseus sets down Medusa's head on the ground and when the Gorgon's blood flows into the sea water, it turns the seaweed to stone, thereby forming the first coral reefs.

EIGHT

Rustom and Sohrab

A Story from Persia

The moon lit up Rustom's chamber as he slept soundly. It had been a long day. He had lost his beloved horse Rakhsh that morning. The famed warrior, who had gone hunting, had left the horse to graze and had nodded off under a tree. When he awoke, he found Rakhsh to be missing.

Rustom had deduced from the footprints that Rakhsh had been captured. He followed the footprints to Samangan city, where the king heard of his arrival and welcomed him to spend the night at the palace.

Now, as Rustom slept, someone opened the door to his chamber. The intruder was careful not to make any noise. As the person inched closer to Rustom, he got up with a jolt.

'Who is there?' he called out, drawing his sword. 'Show yourself or I will chop off your head!'

'Hush!'

Rustom was taken aback. It was a woman!

'Who are you and what do you want?' he asked, lowering his voice.

The shadows shifted and the intruder showed herself under the moonlight.

'I'm Princess Tehmina,' she said, looking him straight in the eye.

'And how may I help you, Princess?' he asked, bemused.

'I've heard of your bravery. The stories don't do you justice,' she replied, a small smile playing on her lips.

Rustom grinned back at her.

'I will not waste any more time in trivialities,' said Tehmina. 'I would like to be your bride if you are willing. I've grown up listening to stories about your courage and I cannot imagine finding anyone better.'

Rustom was surprised by Tehmina's words, but her attitude greatly pleased him. On the following day, Rustom and Tehmina were married.

Rustom spent a few happy weeks in Samangan. By then, Tehmina's father had managed to locate Rakhsh, who had indeed been taken away by a group of drunk soldiers.

Finally, the time came for Rustom to leave Samangan and go back to Zabulistan, his home. 'We will meet again soon,' he promised her.

'I'm with child,' Tehmina told him, staring out of the window as twilight fell.

Rustom was delighted to hear the news, but he told Tehmina that he simply could not stay any longer.

'Take this gemstone, my love,' Rustom said, enveloping her hands in his. 'If it's a baby girl, tie it to her hair and if it's a baby boy, tie it on his arm. A small gift.'

Tehmina took the gemstone from Rustom. She knew that he was a restless man, happiest in battle. When they sat together talking, her eyes would silently count the number of scars on his body—old friends, he called them. So, she let him go, promising to send word when the baby arrived.

The months passed by quickly. Tehmina watched the trees shed their leaves and bloom again, thinking of Rustom and wondering if he too thought about her.

One full moon night, she gave birth to a beautiful boy. As she gazed at Sohrab's innocent face, Tehmina felt tears prick her eyes. He looked so much like his father! But in that very moment, she knew that she would never tell Rustom about Sohrab's birth. No, if she told him, he would take her son away and groom him to be a fighter, just like him. He would expect Sohrab to flex his muscles, spill his blood and give his breath to prove he was a man.

When she had been a mere girl, she had been fascinated by such stories of bloodshed. But now, when she knew what it was to bring a life to the world, she no longer thought death was so glorious.

And so, Tehmina sent word to Rustom that she had

given birth to a girl. Rustom sent back many gifts, but just as Tehmina had expected, he did not rush back to see the baby. However, she tied the gemstone around Sohrab's arm, just as she had promised.

Sohrab grew into a strong little boy, chasing after lambs and climbing trees. He loved to practise with the sword, too. Often, he would sit on Tehmina's lap and ask her who his father was. When would Sohrab see him?

'Soon,' Tehmina would say, running her fingers through his curls.

But there came a day when 'soon' was no longer a good enough answer for Sohrab.

'Tell me the truth,' he demanded. 'I want to know who my father is.'

Tehmina looked up at Sohrab's handsome face, already half-covered with a beard. Her son was no longer a child to whom she could give a sweet and hope he would forget his questions. And so, Tehmina told him about Rustom.

'Rustom? My father is Rustom?' asked Sohrab in disbelief. 'The son of Zal is my father?'

Tehmina nodded. She showed him the gifts that Rustom had sent her when Sohrab was born.

'But why has he sent these little girls' clothes?!' exclaimed Sohrab.

Tehmina told him the truth—the trick she had played on Rustom to keep him away from Sohrab.

But Sohrab barely listened to his mother. He was already

imagining the wonderful moment when he would unite with his father.

'I will find my father,' said Sohrab. 'And I will make him the king of Iran and you the queen!'

Tehmina's heart quaked when she heard Sohrab's words. 'There's more to life than battles and glory,' she said.

'I'm not afraid of death,' he said proudly.

'What do you know of death?' shot back Tehmina. 'When that moment comes, there's nobody, nobody who will not pray for one more day, just one more day to live.'

'I've lost enough time as it is, Mother. Don't stop me now,' he said with impatience.

That night, Sohrab did not sleep a wink. He came up with a plan to find his father and fulfil his promise. He decided to take the help of Afrasiyab, the king of Turan, to battle against King Kae Kaus, the ruler of Iran. He knew that if he could find Rustom anywhere, it would be on the battleground.

Like Rustom, Sohrab too was a fierce warrior. When he arrived in Iran with Afrasiyab and his army, his name spread like wildfire. Here was a man who fought like a lion. A man who knew no fear and could not be stopped.

King Kae Kaus was worried. He did what his advisors told him to—bring in Rustom, their best warrior. Only he could stop this stranger.

By the time Rustom arrived, Sohrab had managed to capture the fort of Sapid and the Turanian army was stationed there. Rustom waited till dusk and sneaked into the enemy camp to find out their strategy. He saw Sohrab sitting with two other men and discussing their plans. One of them was Zindeh-razam, Tehmina's brother. She had sent him along with Sohrab to help him identify Rustom.

But Zindeh-razam's face was in the shadows and Rustom did not recognize him. Noticing a movement from the corner of his eye, Zindeh-razam got up to investigate. Quickly, Rustom killed him in the darkness before he could make a sound. When Sohrab discovered his uncle's death, he realized that an enemy had crept into the camp.

The next day, a furious Sohrab went to King Kae Kaus and challenged him to send his best warrior for a fight. That was, of course, Rustom.

When Sohrab saw Rustom, he felt something stir within him. This was completely new, for he was known to have no mercy at all for his enemies.

'Do you know Rustom?' Sohrab asked hesitantly.

Rustom laughed. 'I'm nobody compared to the great Rustom,' he replied, thinking this would make Sohrab lower his defences.

The fight began. The two of them duelled for hours, their swords clanging and clashing. But if Sohrab was more agile, Rustom's experience helped him stand firm.

At dusk, they stopped the fight and decided to meet again the next day.

Sohrab could not shake off the feeling that he knew this

fighter from somewhere.

'Oh, Mother, how I wish you were here to guide me,' he said, looking up at the stars.

But the next day, too, the older warrior denied that he knew who Rustom was when Sohrab asked him.

Sohrab was the better man in the duel this time. He managed to fling Rustom to the ground and was about to plunge his dagger into his heart when Rustom played a trick on him.

'It's against the rules of war to strike the enemy when you overpower him for the first time,' he lied.

Sohrab was strangely relieved when he heard that. He got off Rustom immediately and let him go, little knowing that Rustom would not show him the same kindness.

For, when the two warriors met again, Rustom pierced Sohrab's heart at the first opportunity, surprising the young man with his deception.

'I don't mind dying,' said Sohrab, gasping for breath. 'But I wish I had at least seen my father once. The brave Rustom.'

When Rustom heard this, he couldn't believe it. He caught hold of Sohrab's arm—and sure enough, the gemstone he'd given Tehmina was tied around it. Rustom's screams rent the air as he held his son's drooping head in his lap.

The young man was at peace. He'd met his father at last, but he realized that his mother had been right all along. How he wished he could live for one more day, just one more day. But it was not to be.

Rustom is Persian mythology's most famous hero. His story features prominently in the 'Shahnameh', a long epic poem written by Ferdowsi, which is also the national epic of Greater Iran. It holds the distinction of being the world's longest epic poem written by a single poet. The story you've just read is a shorter version of the events that lead to Sohrab's tragic death at the hands of his own father. According to legend, when Tehmina heard about Sohrab's death, she was so overcome with grief that she destroyed everything around her that reminded her of her son. She dressed in black and died within a year of heartbreak.

NINE

How Lelawala, the Maid of the Mist, Saved Her People

A Story from the Native Americans

Lelawala's dark hair streamed down her back as she walked to the river. The silence was punctured only by the ripple of the water and the occasional bird call. She sat by the riverbank and let her tears flow.

Just three days ago, her husband had died of an illness. Lelawala had watched his strong body grow weak, his bright eyes turn dull and the breath leaving his body in great rasps. Till the end, she had hoped for a miracle. She had prayed to the gods. She had given him medicine made with the herbs she had picked herself. She had asked the elders of her tribe for help and followed their advice. But nothing helped. He was gone.

'Why do you cry, Lelawala?' asked the fish leaping in the river.

'Why do you cry, Lelawala?' asked the eagle resting on the tree.

'Why do you cry, Lelawala?' asked the wind as it blew all around her.

Or so it felt to Lelawala. She closed her eyes for a moment. Already, his face seemed to grow fainter.

A jab of pain shot through her.

Without thinking, Lelawala set her canoe on the river and got into it. She moved up the river, towards the cliff—the cliff from where water fell like thunder, and if you shut your eyes, you felt like you were in the middle of a storm.

It was a long way ahead, but Lelawala would not give up till she reached the top. Her tunic was drenched, her hair was in disarray. But in her grief, Lelawala noticed nothing. She sobbed freely. Nobody could hear her cry above the deafening sound of the water. She felt free.

'Where are you going, Lelawala?' asked the fish swimming around her.

'Where are you going, Lelawala?' asked the eagle circling above her.

'Where are you going, Lelawala?' asked the wind roaring in her ears.

But there was no fish, no eagle and the wind was deathly still.

The water took the canoe in swirls. Lelawala was afraid, but she knew there was nothing she could do any more. It was too late. She shut her eyes and gave in to the force of the water as it ruthlessly ran towards its escape.

And then, Lelawala was falling. Falling down the cliff, one with the water. She waited for the moment when she would hit a rock. The moment when her skull would burst open like a pod of seeds, spilling its cruel memories once and for all. But instead, Lelawala found a pair of strong arms grabbing her mid-air and holding her tight. In panic, she struggled to break free, but the arms wouldn't let her.

Who was this man? What did he want?

The world turned black and Lelawala was asleep. In her dream, she saw the man sitting next to her and watching her sleep.

'What are you afraid of, Lelawala?' he asked softly.

'Why do you want to leave this beautiful earth, Lelawala?' he whispered.

'Why do you want it all to end, Lelawala?' he murmured.

Lelawala opened her eyes. The man was next to her, staring at her face with a mix of curiosity and concern. He had a wide forehead and kind eyes. His hair was streaked with grey, but his body was still supple and muscular.

'Who are you, stranger?' she asked, shocked to find herself in a cave.

'I could ask you the same question,' said the man, a smile on his lips.

He got up and Lelawala gasped, suddenly afraid. The man's smile widened when he saw her expression.

'I will not hurt you,' he said.

'Tell me who you are!' commanded Lelawala, sounding braver than she felt.

'I'm Heno,' said the man.

Heno? Heno, the god of thunder? Lelawala couldn't believe it. Was she still dreaming? But then, Lelawala realized that no ordinary mortal could have rescued her from the waterfall so easily.

'Why did you do it?' she asked quietly. 'Why didn't you just let me die?'

Heno looked surprised by the question.

Lelawala noticed a shuffling behind Heno. Three young men walked into the cave.

'My sons,' said the god of thunder.

The story came tumbling out of Lelawala. As she spoke, recounting the death of her husband and the way she had been tortured at the thought of a life without him, Heno and his sons listened patiently. By the time she finished, Lelawala felt lighter, stronger.

'You can stay here for as long as you want. Till you feel better,' said Heno's third son.

Lelawala nodded. She would miss her people terribly, especially her father, but she knew she wasn't ready to go back. Not yet.

And so Lelawala stayed with Heno and his sons. The cave behind the waterfall became her home and the strangers, her family. Sometimes, she would gaze down from the edge of the cave, trying to see if she could spot her father or her friends. She would smile thinking about the good times they had together, the games they played and the songs they sang. Heno's son, the youngest one who'd asked her to stay, sat with her sometimes, listening to her stories. Lelawala didn't know what she felt towards him, but her heart trembled when their eyes met.

One night, when Lelawala was watching her village from the cave, she saw a huge serpent winding its way by the river. Under the pale moonlight, the snake moved in and out of the shadows. She watched anxiously as it slithered into a tree hole on the banks of the river. But since it did not appear after that, Lelawala went to sleep, somewhat troubled by what she had seen.

The next day, Lelawala was woken up by distant screams. The village! She rushed to the edge of the cave and looked down. Even from that great height, she could see that the crops in the fields below had turned a ghastly yellow. When she sniffed the air, she could smell death. Lelawala felt tears sting her eyes. She knew now what the serpent had done.

She ran to Heno and told him what had happened. 'I must warn my people,' she said. 'The serpent is poisoning the water!'

Heno did not hesitate. He carried Lelawala through the water and she appeared before her people, covered in mist.

'You must leave!' Lelawala said, her voice shaking in desperation.

The people stared at her, pausing in their lamentation.

Who was this young woman? How had she appeared before them so suddenly?

And then, Lelawala's father recognized her. 'It's Lelawala!' he said, surprised.

Lelawala smiled in joy. She told her people about what she had seen.

'You must move to higher land or the snake's poison will kill everyone,' she said.

The people listened to her, for she was their daughter.

When the great snake wound its way to the river once again, it was angered to see the deserted village. Hissing madly, it slithered towards the people's new home. But Heno would have none of it. The god of thunder sent a lightning bolt crashing upon the snake. The beast was charred to death instantly. But its body was flung across the river, changing the river's course and making the water flow into Heno's cave behind the waterfall.

Heno, his sons and Lelawala rose to the sky together. They would find a new home in the clouds and Lelawala would watch over her people once again, with peace in her heart.

This story is from the Iroquois people and is popularly known as the Legend of the Maid of the Mist. The Iroquois Nation comprises a subsection the Native American people and is also known as the Six Nations Confederacy. The waterfall referred to in the story is the Niagara Falls, which is made up of three waterfalls: Horseshoe Falls

How Lelawala, the Maid of the Mist, Saved Her People 57

(or Canadian Falls), American Falls and Bridal Veil Falls. The popular boat tour in the falls is called Maid of the Mist and is based on this legend. There are different versions of this story, with a popular one that says Lelawala was thrown down the waterfall as a human sacrifice. However, the Iroquois people have objected to this interpretation since their culture does not have such practices.

TEN

Romulus and Remus

A Story from Rome

Romulus and Remus were toddlers when the shepherds found them. Cuddled up against a giant she-wolf next to the Tiber river, the two boys slept blissfully in the still night. The shepherds, who were traveling from one village to another, were surprised that the wolf had not killed them.

When the shepherds approached them, the wolf got up and growled in warning. Her yellow eyes were cautious, but the shepherds knew that any moment, she could pounce on them. The men stopped in their tracks, but by then, the two boys had woken up. Their curiosity aroused, they went to the shepherds and pulled at their beards, laughing when the men cried out in mock pain.

The wolf saw that the men meant no harm and sat down once again. She did not move when she saw the men taking the boys with them. She knew where they came from, where they belonged.

Romulus and Remus thus came to live with the shepherds, who did not know who their parents were. But they often told the boys the story of the she-wolf and how they had found them that night in the forest.

The two boys grew up quickly into strong young men. They loved each other, but they were also rivals.

'Watch me climb this tree as fast as a monkey,' Romulus would tell his brother, scaling up a tree in a flash.

But not to be outdone, Remus would do the same—blindfolded! If Romulus trained the sheepdogs to keep count of the animals in the pen, Remus discovered how to make the cows yield more milk. They even fashioned bows and arrows out of wood and had contests on who could shoot the farthest.

One day, Remus was herding sheep in the valley when he was suddenly surrounded by the king's guards.

'I've done nothing!' Remus declared, but they wouldn't listen.

They accused him of stealing and took him to the palace court, bound in ropes.

At that time, Romulus was away hunting and did not know what had happened.

When he found out, Romulus rushed to the palace, demanding justice. King Amulius would not hear a word of what Romulus had to say, insisting that Remus was the thief who was harassing the people of the kingdom.

'We're not thieves! Though we don't know who our real parents are, we consider the shepherds to be our family and we make an honest living,' asserted Romulus.

King Amulius paused when he heard that. 'You don't know who your parents are?' he questioned.

Eager to establish their innocence, Romulus and Remus told the king how they had been brought up by a she-wolf near the Tiber river, and how the shepherds had found them one night.

But to their surprise, Amulius suddenly looked afraid. His hands trembled and he gripped the sides of his throne. 'I know who you are!' he shouted. 'You're the sons of Mars and Princess Rhea!'

The two young men were taken aback. They were the sons of the god of war and a princess? How was that possible and how did the king know this?

Looking at their blank expressions, the king roared, 'Don't think you can fool me! It was destined that you will end my reign and it was I who placed you both in a basket and set you afloat on the Tiber! I know you have returned to seek revenge!'

Purple with rage, King Amulius made a move to behead Remus with his sword. But quick as lightning, Romulus jumped in and killed the king instead. And then he slashed through the ropes that bound his brother and set him free.

The court was shocked into silence. What had just

happened? But before anyone could say anything, Romulus and Remus sprang to the throne, each brother standing on either side of it.

'You heard from the king who we are. And now that he's dead, we stake our claim to the throne,' thundered Romulus.

Too stunned to raise any objections, the court agreed.

Romulus and Remus were overjoyed. They ran to tell the shepherds all that had happened. Their family was happy for them but also worried about the future. They knew all too well that the brothers would always play a game of one-upmanship. Till then, it was about bows and arrows, cows and sheep. Now it was about the throne. How would it all end?

Sure enough, Romulus and Remus decided that they wanted to build their own city. They wandered together, singing and jousting when the mood struck them, exploring the land that they now ruled. They did not notice that in the bushes, a beast was stalking them. A she-wolf with yellow eyes.

At last, they reached a beautiful place surrounded by hills. However, while Romulus wanted the city to be built on top of the Palatine Hill, Remus wanted it on the Aventine Hill.

'You're just arguing with me because you want to!' said Romulus.

Remus shrugged. 'Don't be childish. This hill is most suited for the city,' he said.

Neither of them could agree, so they decided to ask the

gods to send them a sign.

'There, I can see six vultures circling the sky! I have won,' declared Remus before long.

'Just six? I have seen twelve,' claimed Romulus.

'You're lying!' said Remus angrily.

They squabbled again and stomped off separately. When the shepherds saw the two young men return, their faces dark as thunder, they knew their worst fears had come true.

Though they had not settled the debate, Romulus went ahead and started building a wall around the hill he had chosen—the Palantine.

Remus, who called him a cheat, did his best to stop him. 'This silly wall? It will be breached by enemies in minutes,' he scoffed.

Romulus turned a deaf ear to Remus's rants, but one day, Remus scaled the wall right in front of his brother to show him that he was right all along.

An enraged Romulus drew out his sword and killed Remus. As he fell, Remus thought he saw a giant she-wolf watch them. Her yellow eyes, he could tell, were filled with tears.

Romulus continued to build his city. When it was finished, he named it after himself. Rome.

The image of a she-wolf suckling two human babies is popular even today in Rome. The cave where the she-wolf is supposed to have lived is known as the Lupercal Cave ('lupus' in Latin means 'wolf'). Rome grew to become one of the most powerful cities in the world for over a thousand years. The day Romulus is said to have founded the city, 21 April, is still celebrated as Rome's birthday. This myth may remind you of another story about an insecure king who tried to get rid of a baby but ended up meeting his destiny—the story of Kamsa (or Kansa) and Krishna. Interestingly, in this story from Indian mythology, Krishna is brought up by cowherds before his real identity is revealed.

ELEVEN

How Thor Won Back His Hammer

A Story from the Nordic Countries

Thor, the god of thunder, was fast asleep. In his dream, he was chasing after a white horse that leapt away from his clutches even as his fingertips grazed its silky tail. As he extended his hand as if to grab the animal, he nearly rolled off his bedding.

The god of thunder woke up and laughed to himself, recalling the dream. He got up to drink a glass of water from the pitcher in his chambers. And that's when he saw that the Mjölnir, his mighty hammer, was missing.

For a moment, Thor wondered if he was still dreaming. Then, he roared, shaking the heavens with his fury: 'My hammer is gone! Who has stolen it from me?'

Loki, the shapeshifter, rushed to Thor. Loki was sometimes helpful to the gods and at other times, a troublemaker. But tonight, he was in the mood to assist Thor.

'What happened?' Loki asked.

Thor pointed to the empty space where he always rested his hammer. 'The Mjölnir has been taken!' he exclaimed.

'We must go to Freyja at once,' Loki suggested.

Freyja, the goddess of war and beauty, owned a beautiful feathered cloak that could give anyone who wore it the ability to fly.

Loki suspected that it was Thrym, the lord of the giants, who was behind this. Who else would dare to anger Thor? Besides, he knew that Thrym wished to invade Asgard, and with the hammer, he would be able to win, too!

Thor and Loki hurried to Freyja's abode.

The goddess was seated in her glittering hall, majestic and calm.

'Freyja, will you lend me your feathered cloak? I have lost my hammer and must look for it!' Thor said in agitation.

The surprised Freyja saw Thor's shaggy mane and the distressed expression on his face.

'But of course,' she said, kindly. 'I would have lent it to you even if it were made of gold or silver.'

Saying so, Freyja asked her attendant to fetch the feathered cloak and gave it to Thor.

Loki volunteered to go to Jötunheimr, the kingdom of the giants, and find out if Thrym was indeed behind the theft. He wore the cloak and left Asgard. The sky was grey, as if it was holding back Thor's grief.

When Loki arrived, he saw Thrym sitting upon a mound

quietly, as if he'd been expecting him.

'Welcome, Loki,' Thrym said, his broad shoulders quivering. The giant's eyes were deep as the ocean and he held as many secrets within.

'How are you and how are things at Asgard?' he continued to speak.

Loki raised his hand to stop the small talk.

'You know how things are at Asgard! Have you taken Thor's hammer?' he asked point-blank.

Thrym stared at him for a while and then slowly nodded. 'Yes, I have. The hammer is hidden eight leagues deep under the earth. Nobody can take it from me unless he brings me Freyja,' said Thrym, scratching his head.

'Freyja! You want Freyja as your bride!' scoffed Loki. 'She will never agree!'

'Then tell Thor to forget about his hammer,' said Thrym. He turned away from Loki, as if he was bored of the conversation.

Fuming, Loki flew back to Asgard and told Thor what had happened.

'We must request Freyja to oblige. Otherwise Asgard will fall,' Thor said in desperation.

So, Loki and Thor rushed to Freyja once again.

'Freyja, you must come with us. Wear your bridal clothes. You're to marry Thrym,' said Thor.

Freyja looked at him in amusement. 'Have you lost your senses along with your hammer?' she asked. 'Marry Thrym!

What an idea!'

Thor knelt down on the floor in sorrow.

'But you must, you must!' said Loki. He told Freyja all that had happened.

Freyja listened to the story, her face turning darker with every word.

'And you two will tell me, a goddess, whom I should marry? You two will strike a bargain, as if I'm nothing but a casket of pearls?' she demanded.

'But...' Loki began.

'Say no more and get out of here before I throw you out! Find another way!' screamed Freyja. She was so angry that even the famed necklace of the Brisings, which she wore around her neck, fell to the ground.

Dejected, Loki and Thor called all the other gods and goddesses and told them about the threat facing Asgard.

Finally, one of them, Heimdall, came up with an idea: 'Let Thor dress up in bridal linen and wear the necklace of the Brisings. He must wear a veil over his head, walk like a woman, and put on precious jewels too. This is the best way to trick Thrym.'

While the other gods and goddesses applauded the idea, Thor was far from happy. 'I will look ridiculous!' he wailed. 'Can you imagine me in bridal clothes?'

The gods and goddesses laughed at the image, but they still told him that this was their best shot. When he'd expected Freyja to actually marry Thrym, why couldn't he at least pretend to be a bride for a short while?

'If you keep delaying, the giants will be here soon,' warned Loki. 'There is no time to waste on trivialities.'

So, Thor dressed up as a beautiful bride, wearing soft linens and adorned his limbs with beautiful jewels.

'Why, you look so charming that even I might take you for a bride,' Loki joked. But the sullen Thor refused to crack even a smile.

Loki, too, dressed himself up as a woman attendant to Thor, and the two of them set forth to Jötunheimr.

When Thrym saw the bride riding towards him, he was delirious with joy. The sun was just setting and the sky was filled with orange and a delicate pink that he felt would match the hues of his bride's blushing cheeks.

'Giants!' an exalted Thrym called out. 'Freyja is coming as I commanded. She shall be my bride. Prepare yourselves for the finest wedding that you will ever see!'

The giants couldn't believe their luck. Freyja was going to be their queen! They'd heard about her legendary beauty and power and couldn't wait to see her. But to their disappointment, they couldn't see her face. Not yet.

'She seems so large!' one giantess told another. 'Look at those arms!'

'She's the goddess of war, after all,' the other giantess whispered back. 'Who can wield a sword with dainty arms?'

Thrym had arranged for a mighty feast and the giants

made merry all evening. The two guests, however, did not talk much. Thrym put it down to shyness.

But the guests were not too shy to eat. The bride, especially, seemed ravenous.

Under his veil, Thor devoured an entire bull, eight whole fish, countless pieces of cake and also drank to his heart's content.

'She eats so much!' the giantess told her friend.

'She is the goddess of war, remember?' the friend said in a hushed voice.

The whispers reached Thrym's ears and he too, watched with astonishment, as dish after dish disappeared beneath his bride's modest veil.

'I've never seen a bride eat and drink so much,' Thrym observed, in what he hoped was an affectionate manner. To tell the truth, he was a little shaken by Freyja's appetite.

'Freyja was so eager to come to Jötunheimr and be your wife that she did not eat for eight nights,' said Loki, doing some quick thinking on his feet.

Thrym was so happy to hear this that he bent low to catch a glimpse of his bride's face beneath the veil, wanting to kiss her. But what he saw shocked him so much that he jumped back.

'Why are Freyja's eyes so fierce? I could see fire in them!' he exclaimed.

'Freyja wanted to come to Jötunheimr so badly that she didn't sleep for eight nights,' answered Loki.

Thrym had heard enough. He didn't want to waste a single moment more before he married Freyja and put an end to all the speculation.

'Bring me the hammer to bless my bride. Put it on her lap and let us take our vows,' said the eager giant.

When Thor heard this, he could barely contain his glee. Loki, too, struggled to keep a straight face.

The Mjölnir was handed over to Thrym and the lord of the giants solemnly laid it on the bride's lap.

In a trice, Thor grabbed it and brought it down on Thrym's head. The giant groaned as he fell to his death, his blood splashing on the white linen that Thor wore. The other giants ran away as Thor brandished his hammer.

Asgard was safe. For now.

Thor returned victorious to Freyja and handed back her necklace.

'So you did find another way, didn't you?' the goddess smiled.

Thor is associated with thunder, lightning, storms, oak trees and strength. The Mjölnir was his symbol of power and makes an appearance in several stories. Thor and his hammer are part of the Avengers universe created by Marvel Comics. In the comics and the subsequent film adaptations, the Asgardians are portrayed as an advanced civilization who've discovered more about science than ordinary people. The Mjölnir is destroyed in one of the episodes and replaced with the Stormbreaker.

TWELVE

Amateraśu Hides in the Cave

A Story from Japan

*A*materasu and Susanoo were arguing. Yet again.
Their father, Izanagi, had banished Susanoo from heaven for causing havoc on earth. Susanoo, the god of storms, had killed thousands in his last spell of fury. The rains had poured on earth for days together, bringing down trees and mountains, making the rivers swallow whole villages, and drowning hapless animals and people.

'Enough of your mischief, Susanoo!' Izanagi had bellowed, unable to bear the sight of his creations being pushed to endure so much grief.

Susanoo had tried to plead with his father, but Izanagi's mind was made up.

'You must leave now. You're banished from heaven,' declared Izanagi.

It was then that Susanoo had gone to Amaterasu, his

sister, to bid her goodbye. But the two siblings ended up quarrelling, as they often did. For, when Amaterasu saw Susanoo coming towards her, she immediately suspected that he was out to trick her. Susanoo in the past had done just that, so she had good reasons not to trust him.

'Tell me honestly why you have come,' said Amaterasu.

The golden rays of the sun made a pretty halo around her head, but when she was angered, they would turn into shooting flames. Susanoo knew that only too well. Amaterasu had nearly scorched him when they had fought previously!

'What can I do to make you believe me?' he asked.

Amaterasu thought for a while and said, 'Let's have a contest and see if we're able to judge it fair and square. Without you trying to pull wool over my eyes, like you always do.'

Susanoo protested and claimed that he'd never done so but agreed to Amaterasu's condition. The siblings exchanged their most prized possessions. Susanoo gave Amaterasu his sword, Kusanagi-no-Tsurugi, and she gave him her necklace. Now, they had to make new gods from the objects.

Amaterasu held the sword over her head and chanted incantations. The sun shone brightly around her head as three goddesses dropped to the ground one after the other from the tip of the sharp blade.

Not to be outdone, Susanoo wrapped the necklace, still warm from being on Amaterasu's neck, on his arm and uttered the magic words that would create life. The wind blew strong and hard and the necklace shivered as the gods began to arrive. One, two, three, four and five.

'I have won!' said a jubilant Susanoo. 'Look, I got more of them from the necklace than you did from the sword!'

But Amaterasu shook her head. 'No, the necklace is mine and it is because of that that you got more. This means that my powers are greater than yours,' she said.

Susanoo would not agree. He argued and argued with Amaterasu, growing angrier by the second. But the sun goddess would not back off. She insisted that Susanoo had lost the challenge and must accept that he was less powerful than she was. Susanoo flew into a terrible rage—and one can imagine what happened next. He summoned the dark clouds to the sky and made them pour down on Amaterasu's rice fields.

'Stop!' she screamed. 'You will kill the crops!'

But Susanoo wouldn't listen. He even threw a pony at her loom, on which she spun sunshine, breaking it into half. Amaterasu's attendant ran towards the goddess to protect her from her mad sibling's anger, but Susanoo struck her down with a thunderbolt, killing her instantly. Amaterasu was heartbroken. She could not stand to be around Susanoo any more. Gathering her golden robes, she fled to a cave to grieve.

The sun set on the world. The skies turned grey and then black. The last time Amaterasu had been so upset was when she had fought with her husband, Tsukuyomi. The two of them had shared the sky together, she controlling the sun and him the moon. But Tsukuyomi killed Uke Mochi, the goddess of food, and Amaterasu was furious with him. She called him an evil spirit and split from him, and since then, the two of them never met.

After Amaterasu went to the cave, the world fell silent. The birds on the trees were puzzled. They forgot to sing their music, waiting anxiously for dawn. The giant bears fell asleep, thinking it was winter already. The people panicked—where had their beloved goddess gone?

Though the other gods went to Amaterasu's cave and pleaded with her to come out, she barely heard them. So loud was the sound of her own sobs!

For several days, the world was plunged into darkness. Even Susanoo came to the cave and begged Amaterasu to end her mourning. But to no avail. Finally, it was Ame-no-Uzume-no-Mikoto, the spirit of merriment, who stepped up to bring Amaterasu out of her gloom.

Dressed in flowers, Ame-no-Uzume-no-Mikoto began dancing outside the cave, her little feet springing energetically. She clapped as she sang, moving her delicate hands in the air and asking the other gods to join in. Such was her grace and enthusiasm that the other gods too began dancing. They laughed and clapped along with the happy spirit, picking up the flowers that fell from her body. They even forgot all about poor Amaterasu, who had locked herself up in the cave.

Inside the cave, Amaterasu paused in her crying and

listened curiously to the sounds of the party outside. The tinkling sound of Ame-no-Uzume-no-Mikoto's bells and the loud peals of laughter made her curious. What was going on outside?

She pushed aside the rock that blocked the mouth of the cave and peeped. And when the first rays of the sun hit the earth, which had been wrapped in a blanket of darkness, the gods remembered Amaterasu.

'Amaterasu!' they shouted, hugging her fiercely and refusing to let her go back to the cave. 'Enough now, you must come back with us,' they said.

Amaterasu smiled shyly. But when she saw Susanoo coming towards her, she tensed. Was he going to fight with her again? But Susanoo was contrite. He didn't want to hurt his sister again.

'This is for you,' said the god of storms, handing over the Kusanagi-no-Tsurugi to her. Amaterasu grinned. She pulled her brother into an embrace and kissed his cheek.

'You're forgiven,' she said. 'Now, wherever you go, behave yourself.'

Susanoo said he would try, but of course, he often forgot his promises. And in those days, the rain would threaten to drown the world till Amaterasu pushed away her sibling and took her place in the sky.

Myths and Legends from around the World

Kusanagi-no-Tsurugi is a legendary Japanese sword and one of the three Imperial Regalia of Japan, the others being the mirror Yata-no-Kagami and the jewel Yasakani-no-Magatama. In Japanese folklore, the three symbolize valour, wisdom and benevolence. All three gods, Amaterasu, Susanoo and Tsukuyomi are believed to have been created from Izanagi when he washed his face after unsuccessfully visiting the Underworld to bring back his wife Izanami. Izanami is supposed to have given birth to the many islands of Japan as well as several other gods. She died after giving birth to the fire god.

THIRTEEN

Osiris and Isis

A Story from Egypt

Osiris, the king of Egypt, stood in the garden with his queen, Isis. Though Osiris was smiling and nodding at what Isis was telling him, a long story about the beautiful falcon she had spotted by the Nile when she went there earlier in the day, his heart was troubled. And Isis knew it.

She waited for the moment when he would stop her and speak, but Osiris continued to smile and pretend that he was listening. Finally, Isis could take it no more. She burst out laughing. 'I've been repeating the same story for hours now and you've been nodding along all this while!' she exclaimed.

Osiris started, and looked at her with guilt. 'I'm sorry,' he mumbled.

'What's on your mind? Why don't you tell me?' Isis demanded.

She knew that unless it was something serious, Osiris would not be so preoccupied. He came from a long line of kings who traced their history all the way back to Ra, and was not given to fretting unnecessarily.

'It is Set,' Osiris confessed at last. 'I hear that he wants the throne.'

Isis paused, and then she said, 'Is the information reliable?'

Osiris nodded.

Set was one of the many children of the earth god Geb and the sky goddess Nut, like Isis and Osiris themselves were. They knew what he was capable of. He liked nothing better than to unleash chaos upon the earth. Once, Osiris and Set had got into a terrible fight. Osiris had landed a kick on Set—a kick so hard that it broke Set's leg. Set had never forgiven him for it and had sworn that he would take his revenge one day.

'What are you going to do?' asked Isis.

Osiris shrugged. 'We shall see,' he said, turning away from her.

But Set struck faster than Osiris could act. Over the years, his powers had grown formidable and that night, when he stood in front of Osiris, his sword drawn, his eyes were black and soulless. He had killed the guards and placed the palace under a magic spell.

'I will make sure you never return,' Set said quietly, plunging the sharp tip into Osiris's breast.

As the great king fell, his last thought was about Isis. Would she be able to defeat Set?

Set, too, knew Isis well, and her love for Osiris and Egypt. And so, he chopped Osiris up into forty-two pieces and threw them all across the kingdom.

When it was dawn and the terrible news broke, Isis sat like a stone on her bed, unwilling to open her eyes to a day when Osiris wasn't alive. But, she was the queen. Grief could wait. Egypt needed her. Osiris needed her.

Set may have outsmarted them, but Isis was not ready to give up, not just yet. If she could produce a rightful heir to the throne, then Set's power could be challenged.

Quickly, before Set could capture her, Isis turned into a falcon and soared into the skies. She knew who she could turn to—her sister Nephthys, who was married to Set, but would not say no to her.

When Nephthys saw the graceful falcon fly towards her, she didn't need Isis to explain. Without a word, Nephthys too turned into a falcon.

Meanwhile, Set took over the kingdom. He was furious that Isis had disappeared, but he assumed that she had fled in fear. He had no reason to worry—she was not a queen any more!

Set was so busy ransacking the kingdom and forcing the people to bow before him that he did not notice the two birds flying high in the sky. Occasionally, they would swoop down—as if they had found their prey. Set had better things to do than watch birds.

But Isis and Nephthys were not hunting; they were searching for Osiris's body parts, which had been scattered across the kingdom.

'Don't weep,' Nephthys would console Isis, each time they found a part and Isis's heart broke as if for the first time.

Isis would nod but at night, when darkness cloaked the kingdom and there was nobody to watch, she would turn into the queen again and weep to her heart's content. Her tears flowed into the Nile, making the river swell and flood the land.

At last, the day came when they found all of Osiris's body parts. Nephthys helped Isis arrange Osiris's body as it should be. Isis wasn't crying any more. She stood next to her sister, shoulder to shoulder, and gazed upon Osiris's peaceful face. She almost did not want to wake him.

Nephthys gave her a nudge and Isis smiled faintly. Taking a deep breath, she called out to Thoth and Anubis. The first was a god who was known for his healing powers, and the second was the master of the rites of the dead.

Together, the four of them wrapped up Osiris's body using special, secret procedures. As they whispered and walked around Osiris, their hands working busily, they chanted the ancient magic that would awaken the late king from his deep slumber. It was tiring work, but the four wouldn't stop.

At last, just as the sky had grown dark and the sun had

set, breath returned to Osiris's body. He was alive!

Isis hugged Nephthys in happiness. She thanked Thoth and Anubis for their help. She lay down next to the stirring Osiris and in that moment, lightning flashed from the sky, straight into Isis's womb. Isis smiled. She knew she had won.

Osiris may never wake up fully and rule the kingdom, but his son would. The son who was already growing within her. Horus.

Isis bid goodbye to Osiris. It was time for him to leave. He would go to Duat, the realm of the dead, and become their king.

Isis turned into a falcon again and flew towards the palace, to challenge Set. To fight a battle once again. As the first rays of the sun tinged the sky orange, Isis arrived at the palace, her jaw set, eyes staring straight at Set's terrified face.

It may sound strange that Osiris and Isis were married though they had the same parents. This practice, however, was quite common in the royal families of Egypt because they believed it would keep the bloodline 'pure'. Modern medicine, of course, tells us that this can lead to genetic disorders. There are many versions of the Osiris and Isis story—from why Set was angry with Osiris to what he did with Osiris's body parts and how Horus was born. However, all of them agree that the tradition of embalming or mummifying the dead started with Osiris.

FOURTEEN

Hippolyta and Theseus

A Story from Greece

*H*ippolyta, the queen of the Amazons, was supervising the morning demonstrations of the warriors. The women, dressed in their armour and wielding swords and spears, did not stop as the queen walked among them, raising an elbow here, correcting a stance there.

The sun beat down upon the warriors as they practised, but none of them complained. They were used to the heat just as they were to the rain and the snow. You could not request an enemy to wait for pleasant temperature conditions when they were at your shores, baying for blood. And so, the Amazons were always battle-ready.

As Hippolyta watched her soldiers with pride, she spotted a ship in the distant sea. She frowned. Who was it? Were they coming towards Themiscyra?

She signalled to her commander-in-chief to take note.

There was no reason for alarm, not yet.

'There's a man at the hull, eating an apple,' observed the commander.

'An apple?' exclaimed Hippolyta. That did not sound like an army that had plans to invade.

She took the glasses from her commander and looked. 'It's Theseus,' said Hippolyta, relaxing. 'It's only days since he returned from Crete.'

The news of how Theseus had slayed the Minotaur of Crete had already made its way to Themiscyra. The hero had killed the dangerous creature—half-bull and half-man—by going into the labyrinth where it was kept.

'I wonder what he wants from us,' the commander replied.

Hippolyta shrugged. 'We shall see,' she said.

On the ship, Theseus and his best friend Pirithous, the king of the Lapiths of Larissa, chatted casually as they ate their apples.

'Do you think she will agree?' Theseus asked Pirithous for the hundredth time.

Pirithous laughed. 'I've never seen you be so nervous! To look at your face now, nobody would believe it is the brave king who beheaded the Minotaur,' he teased.

Theseus grinned. 'Well, it's Hippolyta, the daughter of Ares himself. I don't know if she will consider me worthy of her hand,' he replied.

'There's only one way to find out. Ask her,' said Pirithous.

A pair of dolphins leapt in the gleaming sea, trying to race with their ship.

'I see her,' said Theseus suddenly. 'Look, the graceful woman staring right at us. It's her.'

Pirithous nodded. He could see the famous girdle that Ares had gifted his daughter shining around her waist.

'Then wave!' he said, nudging Theseus.

When the ship reached the shores of Themiscyra, Theseus and Pirithous were welcomed by the Amazons. They took the two men to Hippolyta, who congratulated Theseus on his victory over the Minotaur.

'Oh, so you heard about it?' mumbled Theseus, pleased despite himself.

Hippolyta smiled. She didn't quite understand why Theseus blushed so much, but she was flattered by the attention that he bestowed on her. More than once, Theseus told Hippolyta that she was beautiful and the queen thanked him for his compliments.

The Amazons prepared a marvellous feast for Theseus and Pirithous and the guests made merry with music and dance.

'Do it now,' Pirithous whispered in Theseus's ear before sauntering off to join the festivities.

Theseus was still nervous, but he knew that it was now or never. He turned to Hippolyta, who sat beside him, and said, 'Will you marry me? Be the queen of Athens?'

Hippolyta was surprised.

'I know it's sudden,' Theseus continued. 'I've only just got here. I would have loved to woo you the way you deserve, but you see, Athens needs a queen and I could think of nobody better.'

Hippolyta raised her eyebrows. It was an attractive prospect for sure. Athens was a large kingdom, certainly much larger than the island over which she ruled. Becoming Theseus's queen would make her more powerful than ever before. But as she looked at the warrior women who swirled and danced before her, her eyes fell on the calluses in their hands, the cuts on their skin where the sword had kissed them. Could she leave them behind and follow Theseus to his home? She would be honoured and protected in Athens, but would she ever lead an army the way she did now? Her heart broke, just thinking about it.

'I would love to become your queen,' she told Theseus gently. 'But I have my responsibilities here.'

Theseus was shocked. Though he had been unsure of Hippolyta's answer, he had not expected her to reject him outright. He walked away from Hippolyta and sat by himself morosely. Pirithous, who was watching his friend, guessed what must have happened. Hippolyta was sad to see her guests looking unhappy, but there was little that she could do.

Late at night, just as the party was coming to an end, Pirithous gave Theseus an idea.

'Would it be right to do this?' asked Theseus doubtfully

when he had heard him out.

'It's the only way to get her to agree,' said Pirithous.

Theseus had his misgivings, but he decided to listen to his friend. Accordingly, he went up to Hippolyta and said, 'My queen, we will leave tomorrow. But I would like you to visit our ship before that. I have with me some treasures from Crete and I would like you to see them.'

Hippolyta got up immediately. She was happy that Theseus wished to make amends and thinking so, she followed the two men to their ship. As Theseus showed her around, Pirithous stole away from them and set the ship in motion. It was not until Hippolyta noticed the pair of dolphins, who had returned to race with the vessel, that she realized they were at sea.

'What are you doing?' she shouted. 'Where are we going?'

Theseus bowed his head, but Pirithous answered the queen, 'We're going to Athens. We mean no harm. You can marry Theseus once we're there.'

Hippolyta was furious, but there was nothing she could do. She had left behind her weapons and she knew Theseus and Pirithous could easily overpower her in this situation.

'You think you've won, but my warriors will come for me,' she said.

Pirithous laughed in contempt. 'You think a bunch of women can take on Athens? Come on, you should know better than that!'

Hippolyta did not reply. She gazed in the direction of Themiscyra, counting the minutes. How long before the Amazons realized that she was gone?

The commander was the first to notice that Theseus's ship had left the bay. She was surprised that the guests had disappeared without even saying goodbye. Fearing the worst, she looked around for Hippolyta.

'The queen!' she screamed. 'They have kidnapped our queen!'

The warrior women were tired and sleepy after the party but at the commander's words, they became alert immediately.

'How dare they!' they exclaimed. 'We must bring her back!'

The commander nodded.

'They must think we will not fight back. But remember, Amazons, Athens may have the bigger army, but justice is on our side! Fight till the breath leaves your body. Till the last drop of blood spills to the ground,' she said.

'And beyond!' echoed her army.

The warriors wasted no time in setting sail to Athens.

By then, Theseus's ship had reached the kingdom and the king had ordered his men to start preparing for the wedding. Hippolyta had not spoken one word to him in all these hours, but Theseus hoped that her mood would improve after she became his wife. Twilight was falling and by morning, Hippolyta would be his bride.

Theseus went to bed with that thought in his mind, after making sure that Hippolyta was locked away in her chambers.

'Rest well, Queen!' Pirithous had mocked her, before taking the keys with him and telling Theseus not to worry.

But Hippolyta did not sleep. She stood by the window, waiting. At the slightest sound of a twig breaking, she knew that it was time. Her army had come for her.

And indeed, the queen was right. The Amazons arrived at the dead of the night, unnoticed by anyone. Their training was not for nothing. The women moved swiftly, hiding in the shadows and leaping across the streets of Athens like tigers on hunt.

Their queen held a lamp to her face as they approached.

'There she is!' they whispered, overjoyed to see Hippolyta once again.

The commander took the best of the army with her inside the palace. They slit the throats of the soldiers who guarded Hippolyta's chambers before they realized what was happening.

And then, with a slash of her sword, the commander broke the lock that kept her queen captive. Hippolyta was rushed to the ship and before long, the Amazons left Athens far behind.

It was dawn by the time a scream woke up Theseus. It was the chambermaid, who had seen the bodies of the dead soldiers. He didn't have to open the doors to know what had happened.

'Has she fled?!' shouted Pirithous, in amazement.

Theseus shook his head. 'No. She walked out like a queen,' he replied.

In Greek mythology, the Amazons were a tribe of fierce warrior women who lived on an island. There are many famous Amazonian warrior queens, including Hippolyta's sister Penthesilea, who fought the Trojan War. Some say that the Amazons would chop off one of their breasts to draw a bow better, but there's no proof that such a practice existed. DC Comics has a superwoman character called Wonder Woman who is an Amazonian, and a member of the Justice League. According to Wonder Woman's origin story, she was sculpted from clay by Hippolyta.

Churning

FIFTEEN

Maveli Goes Home

A Story from India

Little Maveli sat on his grandfather's lap as he listened raptly to the latter's stories. There was nothing better he liked than to imagine the characters in Grandfather's stories coming to life. His favourite was about Narasimha, the time Lord Vishnu appeared in the form of a half-man and half-lion figure to save Grandfather's life. Prahlada, Maveli's grandfather, had at the time been a small boy and his father, King Hiranyakashipu, had been very angry with him. So angry that he'd wanted to kill him.

'Prahlada!' Maveli's grandfather would scream, imitating King Hiranyakashipu's rage, to make him giggle. His long white beard would tickle Maveli's cheeks as he bent over the little boy, laughing along with him. Maveli's parents, Virochana and Devamba, would look on and smile at the sight, never growing tired of Maveli's delighted squeals.

Grandfather was the kindest asura that Maveli knew. And in his lap, Maveli learnt about the ways of the world, good and evil and everything in between.

When Maveli grew up and became king after Virochana, he was determined to be the best ruler ever. He worked hard to make sure that nobody in his kingdom went hungry. His reign was just and the people couldn't stop praising him.

Maveli knew that his grandfather, who was no longer alive, would have been proud of him. His guru Shukracharya often told him so.

But as the years passed, Maveli grew restless. As he heard tales of injustice from other kingdoms, he yearned to bring those people too under his rule. Maveli had a formidable army and he was an intelligent conqueror who knew just when to strike. Soon, the whole earth was ruled by him.

'But this isn't enough,' Maveli told Guru Shukracharya, who sat next to the throne. 'There's more work to be done.'

Shukracharya looked at him, puzzled.

'There are three worlds, isn't it?' said Maveli. 'What about heaven and the netherworld? Why must I stop with the earth?'

For a moment, Shukracharya was at a loss for words. 'But you will anger Indra and all the other devas,' he finally said.

'The devas!' Maveli exclaimed in scorn. 'They do many wrongs but get away with it because they are devas. And when the asuras do the same, we're branded as evil.'

'You're not wrong, king. But think of the consequences,' Shukracharya said, smiling.

Maveli shook his head. His mind was already made up.

In the days that followed, Maveli unleashed his forces in heaven and the netherworld, conquering both. Indra, the king of the devas, was no match for Maveli's skills, and he was infuriated by the asura's daring.

Defeated in battle, Indra marched up to Lord Vishnu, seeking justice. 'This cannot go on!' he said, flinging his arms in annoyance.

Vishnu was amused but didn't want to upset Indra more. 'Bad day in heaven, Indra?' he asked politely.

'You know what has happened!' said Indra, like a petulant child. 'That Maveli must be shown his place!'

'From what I heard, he defeated you in battle fair and square,' said Indra, suppressing a smile.

'He's grown too big for his sandals,' muttered Indra. 'He has an inflated head, that asura! Don't you see, he is now the king of all the three worlds! He will not be satisfied with this. What if he turns rogue? Too much power in one person's hands is never any good.'

'What do you want me to do?' asked Vishnu.

'Teach him some humility,' said Indra.

'You mean you want to be king of heaven again?' grinned Vishnu.

But though Maveli was a good king, Vishnu knew that Indra had a point. Too many kings with the best intentions had lost their heads once their thrones grew bigger.

Meanwhile, Maveli was set to perform the Ashwamedha Yagya on the banks of the river Narmada under the advice of Shurkracharya. The yagya, which kings all through history had performed to establish their supremacy, would announce to all three worlds that Maveli was unconquerable.

Vishnu watched the preparations with interest. Maveli's magnificent form, as he sat by the river, gazing at the gurgling water, filled him with affection. Perhaps the great king would understand what Vishnu was about to do? After all, he was the grandson of Prahlada, the wise. Being a god was always bittersweet.

And so, Vishnu began to shrink until he became the dwarf, Vamana. Dressed as a brahmin[*] and carrying a wooden umbrella, Vamana walked towards Maveli.

The yagya was about to start but when Maveli saw Vamana approach him, he paused. There was something familiar about this small man, but Maveli couldn't put his finger on it. He reminded him somehow of Grandfather, though he looked nothing like Prahlada.

Before Shukracharya could intervene, Maveli said, 'What do you want?'

Vamana smiled. 'Will you give me anything I want?' he

---

*Brahmin: In the hierarchical caste order in Hindu society, the brahmins are considered to be the highest and often received privileges that were denied to other castes. It's likely that Vishnu took the form of a brahmin man because he may have been stopped from approaching the king otherwise.

asked, a mischievous expression on his face.

Shukracharya and the guards drew their breath. What nerve to speak to the ruler of the three worlds like that!

But Maveli merely lifted his eyebrows. 'I will,' he said. He still couldn't shake off the feeling that he knew this man from somewhere.

'Be careful,' Shukracharya hissed into Maveli's ear. 'He does not seem to be who he claims he is.'

But Maveli's curiosity about Vamana made him brush aside his guru's words of caution. 'Ask!' he said loudly.

'All I want is three paces of land,' said Vamana, putting his tiny foot forward.

The guards burst into laughter, as did the people who'd gathered there to see their beloved ruler, but Shukracharya's face grew grim. 'Don't do it,' he whispered to Maveli, but the king would have none of it.

'Granted,' he said, his eyes drawn to Vamana's peaceful face.

Suddenly, Vamana began to grow in size. The laughter of the guards stopped. Shukracharya's jaw fell open. But what of Maveli? Maveli knew at last who this was. He recognized him from his childhood. The stories Grandfather used to tell him.

With one foot, Vamana covered the earth and the netherworld. With his other foot, he covered heaven. And he still had one pace of land left.

'Where should I keep my foot next?' he demanded.

Maveli knelt down. The people gasped. Shukracharya cried out to Maveli to stop, pleaded with Vishnu to leave him be. But Maveli would not plead for his life. The asura king knew better than to lower his dignity.

'Place your foot on my head,' Maveli told Vamana.

And that's what happened. When the giant foot landed on Maveli's head, he was pushed to the netherworld, the screams of his grief-stricken people echoing in his ears. He knew they loved him and that's what mattered.

Vishnu returned to his abode, the job done. Indra was happy, but the Lord wasn't. He was troubled by what he had done, the pain he had caused to the thousands who had adored Maveli. And so, Vishnu decided to make amends.

'I did what I had to do,' he told Maveli. 'But you can still visit your people. Every year, you may go to earth once to see your land and be with them.'

Maveli smiled. He now had a story just as good as Grandfather's tale about the half-lion, half-man, to tell his people.

Onam, in the Indian state of Kerala, is a harvest festival that celebrates the return of Maveli, also called Bali and Mahabali. People make floral decorations, prepare feasts and dress up as Maveli in honour of the great ruler who once walked their land. The legend of Maveli is also popular among oppressed people whose lands have been taken away by powerful communities because they see the ruler as a hero who was tricked into losing his rightful kingdom.

SIXTEEN

Renuka, the Warrior Goddess

A Story from India

Little Renuka loved the mountains. She knew every rock, every weed that grew in the slopes. She knew when the waterfalls would spring to life, when the tiny fishes would fill the stream and when the rainbow would come out to paint the sky.

Her parents, the mountain king and queen, loved their daughter very much. They watched her grow up among the wild flowers, free as a butterfly that roamed among the bushes. Though they had other children, the spirited little girl was their favourite.

But the day came when Renuka was married to Jamadagni. Jamadagni was a famous sage, but he was also known for his short temper.

Her mother, Jamilika, was worried, as Renuka was leaving her home in the mountains.

'She can take care of herself,' Shiva, the mountain king, reassured his wife.

But Jamilika's heart would not be quiet. Next to his mother, Pothuraju watched his sister walk away. They had been playmates for the longest time and though they often fought, he knew he would miss her smiling eyes.

Years passed.

Renuka and Jamadagni had a son named Parashuram. They were a happy family, though once in a while, Jamadagni would lose his cool for the silliest of reasons and throw around the pots and pans in the house. On such days, Renuka would go to the river and fish, ignoring Jamadagni's tantrums.

One day, an eagle came to Renuka's home with a message from her father. 'The rakshasas have attacked the mountains!' the eagle told her. 'Your parents have hidden themselves in a cave.'

Renuka was startled. She got up immediately, ready to defend her old home. But she remembered that Jamadagni was meditating in the forest. She had to tell him where she was going or he may never find out…if the battle came to that.

'I will take his lunch with me,' Renuka said to herself.

Balancing seven pots of rice and water on her head, Renuka walked swiftly towards the jungle.

Lord Vishnu and Sage Narada were watching the drama unfold on earth from heaven.

'This is a good time to test Renuka, isn't it?' said Narada, mischievously.

Vishnu smiled. Narada was always cooking up pranks and trying to instigate trouble. But Vishnu, too, was bored and in a mood to test Shiva's daughter. So, the two of them disguised themselves as beggars and stopped her on her way.

'Oh, Ma, please give us some food. We haven't eaten in days!' pleaded Vishnu, holding his wrinkled stomach.

'I haven't eaten in years!' wailed Narada.

Vishnu shot him a look, as if to tell him not to overact and give the game away. But the kind Renuka suspected nothing. At once, she put the pots down and served the two men a hearty meal. When they were done, she put the pots on her head again and went to meet Jamadagni.

The sage was just preparing to leave the forest when he saw his wife. 'What are you doing here?' he asked, surprised.

Renuka told him the whole story. But instead of being worried for Shiva and Jamilika, Jamadagni was furious that Renuka had shared his food with the beggars. His eyes burned like coal and in fury, he shouted for Parashuram. Their son was nearby, hunting wild boar, and he came at once when he was summoned by his father.

'Cut off her head!' ordered an imperious Jamadagni, pointing at Renuka.

'What?!' exclaimed Parashuram. 'She is my mother!'

But Jamadagni would have none of it. 'Do it or I will unleash a terrible curse on this earth!' he screamed.

Parashuram turned to his mother with pleading eyes. Renuka's face did not betray any emotion. Her eyes were calm and cold as the deep ocean. She gave a nearly imperceptible nod to Parashuram. His hand shaking, the agonized son raised his sword and brought it down upon Renuka's neck. Blood gushed from the wound in streams. For a moment, even Jamadagni was shocked by what had happened.

Parashuram crumpled to the ground in horror. 'What have I done! What have I done!' he mumbled to himself, groaning like an old man.

And then, before Jamadagni could do anything, Parashuram rose and chopped off his own arm!

But as soon as the arm fell on the earth, mushrooms sprang up in its place. And beside the cluster, there slithered a beautiful, black cobra. It was Renuka!

'I must go to the mountains and help my parents. Turn me back into a woman again,' she hissed.

But the arrogant Jamadagni would not listen. 'You can't order me around,' he said.

Renuka had had enough. She closed her eyes and thought of her mother. The strong Jamilika, who knew no fear. The smell of her warm body enveloped her, as if she were a child running free in the mountains once more. And Renuka emerged in her true form, that of Shakti.

A thousand hands did Renuka have, each of them adorned with weapons sharper than Jamadagni's acid tongue.

'Now? What will you say to me now?' asked Renuka.

Jamadagni spluttered and tried to run away, but Renuka held him by his robes. She didn't need him any more, but Jamadagni gave in to her wish out of fright. Renuka was back to her real form, and she strode towards the mountains with an unflinching gaze.

With a sword in each arm, she fought the rakshasas under the blazing sun. Blood rained on the brown earth, making the mountains look like they were alight. But though she slaughtered the rakshasas, each time their blood fell on the ground, they rose again and fought with new energy. Renuka knew what she must do.

'Pothuraju!' she called out to her brother. Renuka's voice carried over the mountains, past the river and the jungle, to reach Pothuraju. He had not known about the rakshasa attack.

When he hurried home and saw his little sister bravely fighting the rakshasas, he swung into action at once.

'I can take care of them,' panted Renuka. 'I need you to stop their blood from spilling on the ground.'

Pothuraju understood. He put out his tongue and began to lick away all the blood that fell on the earth as Renuka fought the great rakshasas. In minutes, the battle was over. When silence fell over the mountains again, the king and his wife emerged from the cave at last.

'I told you that she can take care of herself, didn't I?' Shiva said to Jamilika.

Jamilika smiled at her daughter's bloodied face, the hands rough with a thousand cuts from the sword, the dishevelled hair framing her proud face. Yes, Renuka could take care of herself. Jamilika's heart was quiet at last.

There are many versions of the Renuka, Jamadagni and Parashuram story. In most of them, Renuka is a submissive and devout wife. Mushrooms are considered to be a sign that the goddess has arrived. Pothuraju, too, is worshipped as an avatar of Lord Vishnu. This retelling is inspired by the version that is popular among the Dalit communities of undivided Andhra Pradesh, where Renuka is celebrated as a warrior goddess. It is loosely based on the story narrated in Vicissitudes of the Goddess: Reconstructions of the Gramadevata in India's Religious Traditions *by Sree Padma (Oxford University Press, 2013).*

SEVENTEEN

How Kundalakesa Became a Monk

A Story from India

From afar, Bhadda's hair looked like a buzzing hive of honeybees. The wild curls swayed restlessly in the wind as she climbed up the trees and swung freely from the branches. In such moments, Bhadda felt she was one with the air, the light, the earth.

Bhadda's mother always worried about her stubborn daughter. 'Tie up your hair!' she would say, every time she saw Bhadda.

Her daughter sometimes obeyed her, gathering up the strands into a bunch and arresting them with a ribbon. But it was of no use—within the hour, Bhadda's hair would tumble loose, escaping the ribbon's clutches. When her mother admonished her again, Bhadda would simply walk away, shrugging her shoulders.

Bhadda lived in a huge mansion in Rajagaha, in the state

of Magadha. Her family was rich, and as if to make up for her mother's strictness, Bhadda's father pampered his daughter as much as he could. He called her 'Kundalakesa', or the one with the curly hair.

From pretty dolls to catapults that brought down juicy mangoes, Bhadda's father fulfilled her every wish. Bhadda surrounded herself with things, big and small, to make up for the emptiness that gnawed at her at times.

But the day would come when Bhadda's father would find it difficult to give in to his daughter's desire.

From her balcony in the mansion where she lived, Bhadda saw Satthuka, the handsome son of the priest. He was tall and had a proud bearing. As he strode down the street, Bhadda felt her heart flutter. She fell in love with him instantly. So much in love, that she did not realize that Satthuka was being led by guards. He was on his way to be executed for cheating scores of people.

When Bhadda at last noticed what was happening, she ran to her father. 'You must help me! You must stop it!' she gasped.

Her father was bewildered. 'What are you talking about, Bhadda?' he asked.

Bhadda dragged her father to the balcony and pointed to Satthuka's retreating back.

'That's the man I will marry!' she declared.

'Him! But he's being arrested,' said her confused father.

'Save him or I will die,' said Bhadda quietly.

Bhadda's mother raved and ranted about her daughter's foolishness, but Bhadda turned a deaf ear. She would not eat or drink till Satthuka appeared before her.

Finally, Bhadda's father managed to bribe the guards and free Satthuka. Satthuka was puzzled. Who was this great man who had come to rescue him in the nick of time?

'My daughter Bhadda wants to marry you,' said Bhadda's father stiffly. 'I know you are not a good man but promise me that you will treat my daughter well.'

Satthuka grinned. He knew there was a golden opportunity before him. Bhadda's father wore expensive silks and precious rings on his fingers. If Satthuka played the game well, he would have an easy life ahead of him.

'Of course,' he said to the uneasy man who stood before him. 'When she has saved my life, why wouldn't I treat her with love and respect?'

Bhadda's father brought Satthuka home to meet his eager daughter.

As soon as Bhadda saw Satthuka, her gloomy face broke into a genial smile. Ignoring her mother's disapproving frown, Bhadda ran up to her room to deck herself in the finest of jewels. She came down, looking resplendent in her new clothes and sparkling gems. Satthuka looked straight into her eyes and smiled. Bhadda did not lower her gaze or blush. She knew she was beautiful and had fully expected Satthuka to be impressed.

'Before we marry, I must make an offering to the cliff

deity. I had prayed that I must be saved from my fate and my prayers have been answered through you. I would be honoured if you accompanied me there,' Satthuka told Bhadda.

Before her parents could respond, Bhadda immediately agreed. So, the two of them set off to the cliff, hand in hand.

'What is it about me that you like so much?' Satthuka asked Bhadda curiously.

'Everything,' said his bride, pulling up the silk from her ankles as she climbed the mountain, her heart singing.

They reached the top of the cliff and Bhadda looked around in surprise. She could not see any temple there.

'Where is the deity?' she asked.

Satthuka began to laugh. 'Foolish woman!' he said, 'Remove all your jewels and give them to me!'

Bhadda's face darkened. At once, she knew what Satthuka planned to do.

'I will, but only if you let me embrace you for the first and last time,' she said meekly.

Satthuka threw his head back and laughed. 'Oh, you're so amusing, I give you that!' he said.

In his mirth, he did not notice that Bhadda had deliberately moved to the edge of the cliff.

'Come to me,' she said, holding her arms wide.

Satthuka walked towards her, still howling with laughter. Bhadda enveloped him in a bear hug. Before Satthuka realized what was happening, she pushed him down the cliff and he fell to the ground with a scream.

The wild wind on the cliff ruffled Bhadda's hair. For a moment, she wished to sit down and wail at her ill fate. But looking at the world from that great height, Bhadda suddenly felt calm. The town looked so small. The people were like ants, scurrying about their business. From the cliff, it seemed to Bhadda that all of her problems were insignificant. Life was much bigger than that.

She removed her jewels one by one and threw them down the cliff. With the edge of a broken knife that she found in the bushes on the mountain, she shaved off her curls. She knew her parents would be shocked to see her like this, but she did not plan to go back home. Bhadda left the mountain and joined the monks. The girl who swung on the trees was forever going to become one with the air, the light and the earth.

Could she, who had lived in silks and slept on soft beds, really lead the life of an ascetic?

Yes, because Bhadda, her father's dearest Kundalakesa, was still stubborn.

Bhadda was one of the earliest Buddhist women monks. Initially, after she left home, she is said to have joined the Order of the Niganthas, a group of monks following Jainism. She learnt the doctrine of the Niganthas and left them. Bhadda was known to be sharp at debates. In her wanderings, she would make a sand pile at the entrance of a city or town and stick a branch from the Jambu tree on it. She would tell the children there to pass on the message that if anyone wished to debate with her, the person should trample on the branch. She would then go to her dwelling and return in a week to see if anyone had taken up her challenge. Eventually, Bhadda met with the Buddha. The latter understood the depth of Bhadda's wisdom and gave her an important place among the female Buddhist monks.

EIGHTEEN

Andal

A Story from India

Little Kodhai was playing with the baby goat who'd followed her home from the temple. It was white, with black patches near its eyes, and Kodhai was delighted that it wanted to stay with her. She fed it grass off her hands and the goat nestled against her contentedly.

'Do you know about my friend Kannan?' Kodhai asked the goat.

The goat didn't think it was necessary to respond. The little girl was rubbing its back, the sun was warm and there was no need to bleat and spoil the peace of the moment. The little girl continued to talk, but the goat didn't mind this. Her voice was sweet and the goat liked listening to her.

'There's nobody like Kannan in this world,' Kodhai told the goat. 'I meet him every day. He plays the flute for me. He's dark as the clouds and his eyes…'

'Kodhai!' called out her father, Vishnuchittar. 'What are you doing there? Did you drink your milk?'

'Yes, I did!' Kodhai shouted back. 'I'm out here in the garden. Come and see my new friend!'

When Vishnuchittar came out to the yard, he smiled seeing the baby goat. 'What have you named it?' he asked, patting his daughter's head.

'Nothing yet,' shrugged Kodhai. 'Appa, I wrote a new poem today about Kannan. Do you want to hear it?'

Of course Vishnuchittar wanted to hear it. As he listened to Kodhai sing, his eyes turned misty. How quickly she was growing up! It seemed like yesterday when he'd found her wailing helplessly under the tulsi plant in his garden. Until then, Vishnuchittar's life had only revolved around Lord Perumal. When he first saw the baby, he considered giving her away to a relative. It would be difficult for him to look after her, he thought. But when he picked her up, the baby gurgled and caught his finger with her tiny fist. Vishnuchittar knew then that he wouldn't be able to part with her.

And so, the little girl grew up listening to Vishnuchittar's stories, his love for the Lord, and above all, poetry. When she was old enough to speak, her first words were about Kannan, Perumal's avatar, and Vishnuchittar was so proud.

'Is it good?' she asked him now anxiously as she recited the last line of her poem.

Vishnuchittar nodded and hugged her tight. Kodhai

laughed and broke free. He was disturbing the goat!

The next day, Kodhai woke up early. She'd promised to take the goat to the mango orchard before going to the temple. It was her favourite place and she wanted to show it to her new friend. But where was the goat? She tiptoed around the house, looking for it, and that's when her eyes fell on the garland that her father had made for the Lord. Made of tulsi, sampangi and sevanthi flowers, the garland smelt so fragrant that Kodhai couldn't help herself. She picked it up and wore it. Ah! How beautiful it looked against her golden-brown skin!

But before her father could see her, she removed the garland and kept it back in its original place. She knew that offerings for the Lord were not supposed to be touched by anyone, but she did not really believe that the Lord would be offended. Her father would be, though!

She loved wearing the flowers so much that since then, Kodhai made it a practice to wear the garland every morning before her father took it to the temple. It was her little secret. Only three beings knew about it—Kodhai, the goat and Kannan.

One day, however, Perumal decided to play a trick on Vishnuchittar. After all, for how long could he let his devotee continue in his ignorance?

So, that morning, when Kodhai wore the garland and kept it back as usual, he made sure that a strand of her hair was caught among the flowers.

When Vishnuchittar offered the garland to the priest at the temple, the latter was horrified. 'This garland has been worn by someone else!' he thundered. 'Look, there's a strand of hair in it. You must know better than to give the Lord a garland that has been used by another.'

Vishnuchittar was shocked and saddened to hear the priest's words. It was true, there was a long strand of hair in the garland, and he had no doubts about whom it came from! Kodhai's hair was so long and thick that she tied it to the side of her head in a bun. The strand could have only come from her.

Vishnuchittar marched home in fury and threw open the doors. Kodhai looked up in fright. She was painting and the colours splashed on the floor.

'How dare you wear the garland meant for the Lord!' he shouted.

The little girl's eyes welled up, but Vishnuchittar was in no mood to calm down. She tried to tell him that she'd meant no harm, she begged and pleaded with him not to be so angry. But Vishnuchittar would not be consoled. He flung the garland away and stomped out of the house.

The next morning, Kodhai lay on her mat and did not get up till her father left for the temple with a freshly made garland.

'He's still mad at me,' she confided in the goat. 'But I know that the Lord is not. He told me so when I asked him.'

At the temple, a flustered Vishnuchittar examined the

garland over five times before handing it to the priest, who glared at him.

'Nobody has worn it, I promise,' Vishnuchittar said.

The priest wordlessly took the garland and attempted to place it on the deity. But no matter how many times he tried, the garland wouldn't sit on the Lord. He gave it back to Vishnuchittar, shaking his head.

'Perhaps the Lord still hasn't forgiven you,' he said.

Vishnuchittar was heartbroken. He walked back home, his eyes on the ground, fervently praying to the Lord to forgive him. 'Kodhai is still very young, she did not know,' he muttered.

When he returned, Kodhai did not come to him as she usually did. She stayed away in the garden, playing with her goat and reciting poetry to the butterflies. The house that was usually filled with Kodhai's laughter was deathly quiet that day.

At night, Vishnuchittar fell asleep after tossing and turning in bed for several hours. In his dream, Perumal appeared before him and asked why he was so troubled.

'Lord, you did not accept the garland from me. It appears that you are still angry,' said Vishnuchittar.

But Perumal only smiled. 'I did not accept it because I missed Kodhai's garlands. Will you please ask her to wear the garland once before you bring it to me tomorrow?' said the Lord.

Vishnuchittar stared at him, agape. And then, tears began

to flow from his eyes. Tears of happiness. Kodhai was no ordinary being. His daughter was one with the Lord himself!

And from that day, Kodhai came to be called Andal—the girl who ruled over the Lord.

Kodhai or Andal is the only woman among the twelve Alvar saints of south India. The Alvars were ardent devotees of Lord Vishnu or his avatar Krishna (known as Kannan in the South) and composed poetry in his praise. Perumal is described as the Supreme Lord in ancient Tamil scriptures and he was later considered to be a manifestation of Vishnu. Andal is believed to have composed the great literary Tamil works 'Thiruppavai' and 'Nachiyar Thirumozhi'. Even today, the garland worn by Andal in the Srivilliputhur Andal temple is sent to the Venkateswara temple in Tirupati during the annual temple festival called Tirupati Brahmotsavam. And for the Andal festival in Sirivilluputhur, the garland from the Venkateswara temple is sent!

NINETEEN

Nandanar

A Story from India

The drum was ready. Nandanar beat it to test if the tone was right. He smiled when he heard the sound—it was perfect, just as he'd expected it to be. The instrument looked so beautiful that he did not want to part with it. But that's how he felt about each drum that he made. The money he'd get by selling the drum would hopefully feed him for the next few days.

Before putting the drum away, he played it one last time. He imagined Sivan moving to the beat in his glorious form as Nataraja, the god of dance. Faster and faster would Sivan swirl, his long locks of hair cracking the air like whiplashes. His eyes closed, Nandanar could feel the tears trickle down his face as he thought about the Lord and his mysterious ways.

Today, he was going with the people of his village to

Tirupunkur, where there was a beautiful Sivan temple. Nandanar got ready and waited impatiently for his family and friends to join him.

'Hurry up,' he said to his neighbour who was still eating breakfast. 'What is taking you so long?'

He dodged a hen and its chicks as he ran down the narrow street, asking everyone to finish their chores quickly.

'All this show for what?' his neighbour muttered to his wife. 'We won't even be allowed inside the temple!'

'Why not?' asked his young son, who was very fond of Nandanar and planned to go to the temple too.

His father shook his head sadly. 'That's the rule. People like us cannot step inside,' he said.

The boy, who was no older than five, did not understand. 'Who made this rule?' he asked, refusing to be distracted by his mother's insistence that he eat something.

'That's the way it's always been,' replied his father. 'Why don't you ask Nandanar?'

When at last he'd managed to rouse everyone in the group that was going to Tirupunkur, Nandanar picked up the little boy affectionately and asked, 'Ready?'

The little boy nodded and then said, 'Will you take me close to the deity?'

Nandanar's face fell. He hated to disappoint the boy, but he could not bring himself to lie. 'No, I can't do that. But we can see the Lord from outside,' he said.

'Father says that's the rule. But why is it so?' questioned the child.

Nandanar didn't know what to say. How could he explain to the boy that people around him thought that those like him could not even be touched? That the temple would have to be purified if he stepped inside it?

'It is late, let's go,' he said, brushing the tears away from his face.

'It's not fair!' shouted the boy, running after him.

The group walked to the temple, talking and singing along the way.

With each step that he took, Nandanar felt his love for the Lord grow. The little boy, tired out by the long walk, was silent. Nandanar made a mental note to give him a present when they returned home. Maybe a spinning top or a catapult?

When they reached the temple at last, the group stood outside reverently and prayed.

Nandanar was right in front and he closed his eyes, picturing the Lord.

'I can't see anything!' said the little boy. 'That big bull is blocking the way!'

Nandanar opened his eyes. Indeed, the Nandi was between them and the deity.

'That big bull's name is Nandi. He guards Kailasam, where the Lord lives. Sivan also travels sitting on Nandi,' Nandanar explained.

The boy looked at the stone bull in wonder. 'He sits on *this* bull? Can I touch him?' he asked.

Nandanar shook his head. 'No, the rules don't allow us,' he said.

Just then, another group of devotees walked past them and entered the temple. Some of them smirked while others screwed up their faces in disgust.

The boy watched as they went inside the temple, crossing Nandi and beyond. 'And they have different rules?' he asked.

Nandanar nodded. He shut his eyes again, pained by the boy's questions. Questions that had come to him too as a child. The times when he had been chased away from temples and told he was not worthy enough to see the Lord. He thought he'd resigned himself to his fate. But the boy's words rankled, reminding him that he'd not forgotten after all.

Nandanar prayed to Sivan, willing the Lord to listen. Sivan heard him all the way up in Kailasam. He felt the ache in Nandanar's heart. How could he ignore his favourite devotee?

'Nandi, you must make way,' he told the bull gently.

'How can I do that?' asked Nandi. 'I must always sit facing you, is that not so?'

'You can make an exception in this temple,' Sivan said. 'How can I deny Nandanar what he asks for?'

Nandi looked at the man with closed eyes and the curious little boy next to him. And sighing, Nandi moved.

In the temple, the people watched in shock as the giant stone bull moved to the side.

'What is happening?' the priest shrieked as the devotees ran out shouting, 'Earthquake! Earthquake!'

But Nandanar did not move an inch. He knew that the Lord had heard him.

The little boy laughed and clapped. The stone bull no longer blocked his view. Before him, rose the mighty form of Sivan, the crescent moon in his hair, the trishul in his hand. And his eyes looked right at him.

The little boy thought the Lord looked pleased.

Nandanar was one of the sixty-three Nayanar saints who were devoted to Lord Sivan or Shiva. Hindu society is built on caste hierarchies and Nandanar belonged to a caste group that was considered to be 'untouchable'. This meant that people belonging to such caste groups were barred from entering temples, could not draw water from wells used by upper-caste people, could not go to schools and so on. Even though practising untouchability is against the law in India today, such incidents continue to happen. The term 'Dalit' is a political identity used by people who have faced such oppression historically. Nandanar was the only Nayanar saint who came from this social background. Even today, the Nandi in Sivalokanathar Temple in Tirupunkur appears on the side and is not in line with the deity, as is the case in other Sivan temples.

TWENTY

Sinhabahu

A Story from Sri Lanka

*P*rincess Suppadevi woke up sweating. It was the same nightmare again. So vivid that she could still feel the hot breath of the lion on her neck. She gulped down a glass of water and tried to sleep, but every time she closed her eyes, the beast sprang towards her. Its giant paws rested on her chest and the golden-yellow eyes looked into hers. And there was no mercy in them.

Were these just dreams or should she be more concerned? Perhaps it was a warning from the gods about what was to come? She decided to tell her father, the ruler of the Vanga kingdom, about it the next day. He would know what to do.

But just as she fell asleep again, a purr reached her ears. And this time, Suppadevi knew that it was no dream. The lion was really in her chamber.

'Let me go!' she screamed as the beast dragged her out to the balcony.

'Hush!' it replied, much to her shock. 'I'm not here to kill you.'

It was a cloudy night and the lion's mane fluttered in the breeze.

'I've watched you for a long time,' the lion said. 'And I'm in love with you.'

Suppadevi did not know how to respond. She felt nothing but fear in her heart. But she was clever enough to know that if she told the lion this, it wouldn't take him long to bite her head off. And so, Suppadevi allowed herself to be carried away by the lion. Dazed by the ordeal, she lost count of the days and nights as the agile beast dragged her through stony paths and narrow streams, finally reaching its cave in the deep jungle.

'You will live here and be my queen,' the lion said, placing her gently inside the cave.

Suppadevi said nothing, but in her mind she was already planning her escape. Her chance would come when the lion went hunting, she thought. But the lion was far more cunning. Every day, before it left, the lion placed a giant rock over the mouth of the cave. Suppadevi did her best to push against it but it was of no use, the rock simply would not budge.

At first, Suppadevi turned away from the lion every time it came near her and tried to be friendly. 'Let me go!' was all that she said. But she soon realized that this strategy wasn't helping her. The lion simply denied her food and she was left hungry till she felt faint.

And so, Suppadevi accepted the lion as her husband. The beast was thrilled, thinking that it had at last convinced her of its love. Little did it know that Suppadevi had not given up on dreaming of her freedom.

In time, Suppadevi gave birth to twins. She called the son Sinhabahu and the daughter Sinha Seevali. The lion was an affectionate father, but it never allowed the twins to step outside the cave. They were shut inside along with their mother, who'd grown thin and weak in the passing years.

'There's a whole wide world out there, do you know?' Suppadevi would tell her children when the lion went out hunting. 'There are as many flowers as there are butterflies. There's the sun and the rain and the snow too. And oh, do you know how beautiful the golden moon looks?' she would say.

Sinhabahu and Sinha Seevali would listen to their mother, round-eyed. When could they go to see all these wonders, they would ask.

'Soon,' Suppadevi would say, gathering them in her arms.

Sixteen years passed thus. Sinhabahu and Sinha Seevali were no longer babies. They knew what their father actually was and they yearned to see the world outside.

'Maybe we can kill him,' Seevali said one day. 'There's three of us and only one of him.'

Suppadevi smiled but shook her head. 'He's far too powerful. He's old now but remember, he has the teeth and claws that we don't.'

'We must escape,' said Sinhabahu, sitting down next to his sister. 'This rock, we must break it.'

Wordlessly, Suppadevi held out her hands. They had callouses all over, from years of pushing against the rock.

'But we are young and we are strong. We will do it,' Sinhabahu assured her.

And so, every day after the lion left, Sinhabahu and Seevali would push against the rock until one day, it finally gave in and the cave fell open.

Suppadevi put her hands to her eyes. The light was too much to take after so many years. But her heart sang with pride. Mother and children wasted no time in running away from the cave. They walked for days on end, frequently doubling back and scattering to put the lion off their scent. At last, they reached the Lala kingdom, where Sinhabahu built a hut for them at the edge of a village.

Seevali, who'd been collecting flower stalks all through their journey, dug the soil and planted them. 'The butterflies will come soon, Mother,' she said.

When a week passed and there was no sign of the lion, the three thought that they had fooled him. But on the eighth day, they heard disturbing news. A ferocious lion had entered the kingdom and was killing everything in sight.

Sinhabahu knew what he must do. When he set out for

the palace, Seevali gave him an arrow that she had fashioned. 'It's dipped in poison I gathered from the plants,' she said.

Suppadevi watched her son leave anxiously, but Seevali assured her that Sinhabahu would be victorious.

When Sinhabahu offered to hunt the lion, the king did not think twice. He gave him all the assistance that he needed, and Sinhabahu went into the jungle to hunt the beast.

It was a bright day, but the jungle was strangely quiet. The monkeys did not chatter as they usually did. There was no birdsong, and even the insects and frogs were silent. In the stillness, Sinhabahu could hear only one sound—the breath of the lion. Suddenly, he saw a shadow move and whipped around. It was his father, the beast growling at him with malice.

'Drop the arrow and tell me where your mother and sister are,' the lion said.

When Sinhabahu shook his head, the lion leapt towards him with an earth-shattering roar. And that's when Sinhabahu shot the arrow and pierced the beast's heart. The lion fell back in shock, the light fading from its eyes.

In the village, Seevali grasped her mother's hand and said, 'Look, Mother, the butterflies. They're coming!'

Suppadevi was from Vanga, which is the present-day Bengal region. Her son Sinhabahu became a hero after killing the lion. He built a city called Sinhapura and married Seevali. Yes, it was not uncommon in those times for a brother to marry his sister. The two of them had a son called Vijaya. There are different versions of how Vijaya reached Sri Lanka, but he is the first recorded king of the island. His rule is traditionally dated to 543—505 BCE. It is said that Vijaya had a lion on his flag, depicting freedom and hope, and the Sri Lankan flag even today has the symbol.

TWENTY-ONE

Cassandra's Prophecy

A Story from Greece

Cassandra hid in the royal stables, waiting for her friends to find her. In the distance, the little girl could see her brothers Hector and Paris duelling. It was a quiet morning and Cassandra nearly fell asleep as she watched the horses gently chewing the hay.

'Caught you!' called out her best mate, tugging at Cassandra's plait.

'I told you she would be there, didn't I?' said Helenus, her annoying twin.

'That's not fair!' shot back Cassandra. 'You're not allowed to help her.'

Helenus merely shrugged and ran away.

Cassandra was angry with Helenus but only for a minute. She loved him so—how could she not? The two of them had been together ever since she could remember, learning to crawl, walk and talk at the same time.

She went to her father, King Priam, who sat in the balcony eating a bowl of grapes. His hair, she noticed, was turning entirely white.

'Cassandra, is that you?' the king said, without turning.

She came towards him shyly and sat on his lap, accepting the fruit when he offered it to her.

Queen Hecuba, her mother, joined them after a while. The three of them sat together chatting about what Cassandra had learnt from her teachers and her numerous complaints against Helenus. Priam threw his head back and laughed, sometimes patting her affectionately when she said something clever.

When she grew silent, Priam followed her gaze, which rested upon the temple of Apollo.

'Do you have any questions, young lady?' asked the king.

'Why do we pray to Apollo?' asked Cassandra.

'Because he knows the past, protects the present and can see the future,' said Priam.

'He's the sun god, isn't he?' said Cassandra, turning to her mother.

Hecuba nodded. 'Yes. And of archery, music, dance, poetry, healing...'

'I want to meet him,' said Cassandra. 'I want to learn everything that he knows! Especially to look into the future. How exciting!'

Hecuba chided her, but Priam only smiled. 'She's a child.

I'm sure Apollo knows better than to shower his wrath on her,' he said.

Cassandra never forgot the conversation. She was a curious child and of all of Apollo's powers, his ability to predict the future fascinated her the most.

'Imagine,' she told her dolls. 'Imagine if I could look into tomorrow and the day after and the day that comes after day after... I would know what I would eat, where I would go, who I would meet. I could find out who would win in the games we play!'

She stared at herself in the mirror, her dark eyes shining. 'Why, if Troy were to go to war, I could even tell Father the moves that the enemies would make! I would save so many lives!' she whispered to herself.

The idea took root in her mind and grew day by day, as Cassandra made daily visits to the temple. She made her offerings and worshipped Apollo with more sincerity than anyone else who set foot in the temple. Priam and Hecuba were amused, but they did not dissuade their daughter. At times, Helenus went with her, but she never told him her secret. No, not even Helenus could be trusted with it.

The years passed. Cassandra grew into a beautiful young woman. She was no longer running around the palace gardens and hiding in the stables, but she still went to the temple of Apollo every single day.

At times, she wondered if Apollo even existed. She had murmured her desire to see him so many times, standing before his image, but the god had not given her a single sign that he was listening. But just as quickly as this thought popped into her mind, she would apologize to Apollo and continue with her worship.

One day, Cassandra had just finished making her offering and was about to leave the temple when she saw a handsome young man watching her. She felt strangely drawn to him, though she did not know who he was. Did he not know that she was a princess? How dare he look at her like that? When she kept walking, he put out his hand and said, 'Do you not know who I am?'

Cassandra looked at him again closely, frowning. There was something familiar about him. Was he an old playmate? Perhaps the prince of another kingdom she had met on their travels?

The young man was smiling, enjoying her confusion.

'No, I don't know who you are,' said Cassandra brusquely, irritated that he was amused.

'Ah! You pray to meet me for years and when I come before you at last, you push me away!' laughed Apollo, for that's who he was.

Cassandra's mouth fell open. 'Apollo! I do not believe it!' she said. And yet, she knew it to be true.

She was overcome with happiness and could barely speak.

'Here I am...' said Apollo. 'Are you going to talk at all or are we just going to stare at each other all day?'

Cassandra smiled. 'I... I have waited for this moment for so long that I don't quite know what to do,' she confessed.

'Well, why don't you tell me what is it that you want? There must be a strong reason why you have been praying so hard,' said Apollo.

'I want to be able to tell the future,' blurted out Cassandra. 'I want to look ahead and know what's to come.'

Apollo whistled. 'Are you sure about this?' he asked.

Cassandra nodded.

'To know the future could take away your present,' warned Apollo.

But Cassandra wasn't listening to him. He could see that she wouldn't be discouraged.

'All right,' he said. 'I will give you the gift of prophecy, but will you stay here with me till daybreak?'

Cassandra didn't think twice. She made the promise and Apollo sighed. He gave her the gift, but the minute he did so, Cassandra fled the temple, not turning when Apollo shouted after her.

'Don't you dare break your promise!' he yelled.

Cassandra did not stop. She ran all the way to the palace, unable to contain her joy.

When she saw her brothers, Hector and Paris, duelling, she closed her eyes for a second. She saw that Hector would win but not before he cut Paris in the arm by mistake.

'Stop. Stop at once. You're going to hurt Paris,' she told her brothers confidently.

But they only laughed.

'Run away, Cassandra, and let us be. Or find Helenus if you're looking for someone to trouble,' said Hector.

Cassandra was furious, but she held her tongue. She would simply wait for the incident to happen and *then*, everyone would know that she wasn't lying. She didn't have to wait for long.

'Ouch!' screamed Paris as Hector's sword sliced his arm.

'See, I told you!' jumped up Cassandra. 'I can tell the future! I really can! I have the blessings of Apollo!'

But the brothers only laughed even more.

'That was a mere coincidence. Go away, Cassandra! You're beginning to sound like a mad woman,' they said.

Cassandra's heart quailed. Suddenly, she knew what Apollo had done to punish her. She would be able to see the future, but nobody would ever believe her.

The future of Troy flashed before her eyes. Soldiers... soldiers everywhere. A giant wooden horse being rolled down the streets. Fire. Death. The wails of the women and children.

'Stop!' she screamed. 'Danger! Danger is coming our way!'

But nobody listened.

In some versions of the myth, Cassandra falls asleep in Apollo's temple and the snakes lick her ears. This gives her the power to hear the future. In the epic Iliad, which tells the story of the Trojan War,

Cassandra is a tragic figure who predicts the destruction coming her kingdom's way, but is never believed. She even warns the Trojans about the hollow wooden horse that is sent to them as a gift by the Greeks—which actually contains soldiers who are ready to attack. Her father Priam at times locks her up because he believes her to be mad. She is also said to have taught Helenus the art of prophecy. In modern times, her name is used to refer to a person who speaks the truth about the future but is dismissed by others. Women's rights activists also use the Cassandra story to illustrate how women's talents are seldom given due acknowledgement.

TWENTY-TWO

Scheherazade

A Story from Arabia

Shahryar, the sultan of Persia, watched as the axe fell on his new bride's neck. She was beautiful, just like the others. His thousandth wife, now no more.

He walked away, already forgetting her face. He tried not to remember their names either.

Another pair of eyes too was watching the execution. Dark and blazing, the eyes did not flinch as the blood spilled on the ground, pooling beneath the body that lay lifeless.

If she had a sword, she would have challenged the sultan and plunged the sharp edge into his brutal heart. She hated standing by and doing nothing while woman after woman was killed in plain sight and no one, absolutely no one, would question the sultan. Not even her father, the vizier.

'Scheherazade!' he hissed when she brought up the sultan's crimes in their home. 'It is against the law to speak ill of the sultan!'

'Then that law must change,' Scheherazade shot back. 'How can you continue working for someone who is so cruel?'

She knew what her father was going to say before he said it—Shahryar had not always been like this.

A few years ago, the sultan had married a charming princess from a neighbouring kingdom. The festivities went on for days, but at the end of it, the bride went missing. She had run away with another man, a commoner whom her father had not allowed her to marry. Shahryar was heartbroken. He thought he could hear the world laughing at him. He sent his men after the princess, but they never found her.

And that's when Shahryar made a terrible oath. He would marry a woman every day of his life and behead her the next day so she would never get a chance to be unfaithful to him.

'He was kind and brave. The best of men. You know that,' the vizier told his daughter, trying to convince her.

Scheherazade scoffed. 'Stop singing his past glories! He has killed a thousand women and you think there's nothing wrong with that?' she bellowed.

The vizier looked around in fear. If anyone heard her, she would be chained and taken away to the sultan. He had no doubts about what would happen after that. He watched with a heavy heart as Scheherazade flounced out of the drawing room. His hot-headed daughter, who loved books and spoke seven languages! There was nothing that she did not know. She could debate philosophy with the wisest of men; she could tell the little children why the stars blinked and why the moon never stayed the same; she could paint surreal worlds in a matter of minutes. And her poetry! How she could write!

The vizier had the greatest love for Scheherazade, but he also feared her tongue. Mostly because he knew she spoke the truth.

Scheherazade could barely breathe as she sat on the swing, trying to calm her mind. Her father was afraid of the sultan, she knew. Earlier, when the sultan had first started this cruel practice, she'd pleaded with him to speak to the sultan. But by now, she knew that the time would never come.

In her room, she had a list of all the women who'd fallen dead in the palace. The kingdom pretended not to see or remember, but Scheherazade would never forget.

'What are you thinking about?' came a voice.

It was Dunyazad, Scheherazade's sister. The one who listened to her mad ideas and never told her to stay quiet.

'I was thinking about...' began Scheherazade.

'The women?' asked Dunyazad. She looked a lot like Scheherazade, except that her hair was not quite as full of wild curls as her older sister.

Scheherazade nodded.

Dunyazad sighed. She, too, felt awful about what was happening, but what could they do about it?

'Let's leave that aside for a while,' she implored her sister. 'Tell me a story, Scheherazade. My head hurts and I want to fall asleep.'

Scheherazade smiled. Dunyazad loved listening to stories—from the time they were little girls, Scheherazade would tell her all about the magical creatures and wonderful places she came across in her books. Dunyazad was too lazy to read the books herself, but she would pester Scheherazade to tell her all about them.

Her head resting on Scheherazade's shoulder, Dunyazad's eyes closed as her sister began telling her a story: 'Once upon a time, there lived a giant...'

But when Scheherazade stopped, thinking Dunyazad had fallen asleep, she woke up immediately and said, 'No, do go on! This story is so interesting that I cannot sleep till I hear how it ends!'

Scheherazade laughed. And that's when the idea struck her. Leaving behind a bewildered Dunyazad, she ran inside the house to find her father.

'Father! I know what I must do! I have it at last!' she said.

The vizier was taken aback. Scheherazade, his deeply thoughtful daughter, was seldom so excited.

But when he heard her out, he was shocked. 'No! I will never allow it!' he said, pushing her away.

But Scheherazade's mind was made up. 'Come and

watch the execution tomorrow with me, Father. And tell me if you still won't agree,' she said, sticking her chin out.

The vizier could already hear the tinkling music from the palace—Shahryar was getting married, yet again.

The next morning, Scheherazade dragged the vizier to the tree from where she usually watched the executions. The vizier tried to cover his eyes, but she forced him to watch.

'What do you say now?' she asked. 'Do you still think I must not do it?'

The vizier did think so, but he knew Scheherazade could not be stopped. And so, he took her to meet the sultan.

'My king, this is my daughter, Scheherazade. She...she has...' the vizier said, unable to complete the sentence.

'I would like to be your bride, sultan,' said Scheherazade.

Shahryar was startled by how bold Scheherazade sounded underneath her veil. The women he'd married so far were so afraid, knowing the fate that awaited them. But here was one who actually wanted to marry him!

'All right,' he said, amused. 'Make the arrangements!'

The vizier was in tears by the time the wedding was over. He was too distracted to notice the two sisters whispering to each other.

After the ceremony, Scheherazade went to Shahryar's chamber. But before he could speak, she said, 'My king, I know that tomorrow I will die. I have only one wish. Could I say goodbye to my beloved sister? I love her dearly.'

Shahryar nodded.

'It will take a while, as I have to tell her a story. She loves listening to my stories and this will be for the last time,' said Scheherazade.

Shahryar was intrigued. 'I will come along, too,' he said, just as Scheherazade had hoped.

So, the two of them went to Dunyazad, who was waiting in the courtyard.

Scheherazade sat down next to her and began telling the story. It was about a genie who was caught in a bottle. Scheherazade described the genie's frustration at not being able to get out, how he began to forget, little by little, of the outside world. How his heart grew old and his anger became the only thing that kept him alive.

'And then, one day, a fisherman found the bottle...' said Scheherazade.

The sultan and Dunyazad leaned forward eagerly. What would happen next?

But Scheherazade stopped. 'It is very late and I'm tired. My voice is weak. I can't go on,' she said.

'But I want to know what happens next!' said the sultan.

Scheherazade shrugged. 'I have no time left,' she said simply.

Dunyazad placed her hand over her sister's, her heart quaking. This was the moment that would decide whether Scheherazade's plan had worked.

'Hmm...' said the sultan grudgingly. 'Well, I can't execute you without knowing how this story ends. I will never have any peace otherwise.'

And so, Scheherazade lived another night. And then another. And then another. For every night, she would tell a story and stop just as it became exciting. The sultan would be persuaded to spare her for one more day, just so he could listen to how the story ended.

Scheherazade told the sultan a thousand stories like this. When the last story was over, she said, 'That's all the tales I know, king. Tomorrow, I will prepare to die.'

But Shahryar would have none of it. In the thousand nights that he'd listened to Scheherazade, the tyrant's heart of ice had slowly melted. Scheherazade had told him great stories about greed, jealously, anger, rage, love, hope and above all, compassion.

Shahryar knew that if he silenced her, the brilliant world she had built for him would come crashing down. And what would he be then, but once again a twisted man, who couldn't bring himself to look at the mirror?

One Thousand and One Nights *or* Arabian Nights *is a collection of folktales from the Middle East, which was compiled in Arabic between the eight and fourteen centuries. There is no single author for the stories and these tales come from different parts of the world—Arabia, Persia, India, Greece, Turkey and so on. The collection follows a story-within-a-story format, also known as a 'frame story'. The stories are told by Scheherazade to Shahryar and each story ends with a brief conversation between the two where she piques his curiosity and he allows her to live for another day. 'The Fishermen and the Genie', mentioned in this story, is one of the popular tales that figures in different versions of* **Arabian Nights**.

—⚬⚬⚬—

Acknowledgements

I thank all the storytellers who came before me, those who fashioned the many versions of the same tale, wrestling with the characters, their conflicts, and what justice they must meet. Those who told the stories, those who remembered them, those who changed them and those who wrote them down. I referred to multiple sources for the stories in this book, making them my own by shifting the perspectives, at times introducing new elements and linking the themes to our current world. Some of these stories, like the one about Renuka, are not commonly known, and thanks are due to researchers/historians such as Sree Padma for taking the effort to document them.

The ownership of a myth does not lie with a single person; it belongs to anyone and everyone, any place and every culture. It is this diversity that allows an affectionate irreverence, though the stories we tell are about the gods.

Thanks are also due to the editorial team at Rupa Publications, who trusted me with this book and kept an open mind to the kind of stories I wanted to tell, and how I wished to tell them.

My colleagues at The News Minute, for their support and love.

My parents, Usha and Rajendran, who never said no to my requests for books, and let me acquire two supposedly useless degrees (BA English and MA Gender Studies) in peace, when the rest of the world was busy in the pursuit of Engineering.

My brother Surjeet, for telling me when my writing sucked.

My husband Magesh and daughter Adhira, for teaching me that life's biggest question is 'What are we going to eat?' and nothing else matters, really.